Money Stability

How to Build Financial Control in an Unstable World

MARK ELLISON

PERENNIAL PUBLISHING

Published by Perennial Publishing

First Edition

Paperback ISBN: 978-971996-03-5
Hardcover ISBN: 978-971996-04-2
EBook ISBN: 978-971996-05-9

For bulk or institutional orders, contact Perennial Publishing.

Contents

The Architecture of Financial Control

Income magnitude is the most visible variable in personal finance. It is the number people cite, compare, defend, and aspire to increase. Yet magnitude is not architecture. A large income can sit inside a fragile structure, while a modest income can operate within a durable one. The difference is not motivational or behavioral. It is structural.

Financial control is not determined by how much flows into the system. It is determined by how that flow interacts with obligations, timing, rigidity, and sequencing. Income is a stream. Stability is a configuration.

Two professionals can earn the same annual salary and experience radically different levels of control. One may feel constant compression despite high earnings; the other may operate with calm latitude at a lower level. The distinction emerges not from discipline or intelligence but from structural design. When inflows, obligations, and timing are arranged without regard to variance, the system becomes sensitive. When they are configured with sequencing tolerance in mind, the system absorbs disruption.

The foundational shift in this chapter is simple: income magnitude is not the primary determinant of financial stability. Structural configuration is.

Financial systems are defined by flows and fixed points. Income represents variable inflow. Obligations represent scheduled outflow.

Stability depends on the spacing, sequencing, and rigidity of those flows relative to each other.

Most instability does not arise from dramatic shocks. It emerges from minor misalignments between inflow timing and obligation sequencing. This is timing coupling.

Timing coupling occurs when income arrival and obligation deadlines are tightly synchronized with minimal buffer. A paycheck arrives on the 1st. Rent is due on the 1st. Credit card payment is due on the 2nd. Insurance auto-drafts on the 3rd. Each obligation assumes exact inflow timing. The structure functions only if the schedule performs precisely.

Under perfect conditions, this configuration appears stable. The bills are paid. The account returns to near zero. The cycle repeats. The system is operating, but it is tightly coupled.

In tightly coupled systems, small delays propagate. A payroll processing delay of forty-eight hours does not reduce income magnitude. It disrupts sequence. The rent payment is late. A fee is triggered. The credit card auto-draft fails. A secondary fee is triggered. Cash position degrades. The system is now compensating for structural fragility, not income shortage.

Sequence sensitivity under minor variance is the defining characteristic of unstable financial architecture. It does not require job loss or medical emergency. It requires only slight deviation from expectation.

Consider two identical earners paid biweekly. The first schedules all fixed obligations within three days of each paycheck. The second staggers obligations across the full pay cycle. Both have identical annual income and identical annual expense totals. The difference lies in sequencing density.

In the first configuration, outflows cluster immediately after inflow. Available liquidity is compressed early in the cycle. The system runs near constraint for the remainder of the period. In the second configuration, outflows are distributed. Liquidity remains available deeper into the cycle. The second system tolerates timing variance more effectively even though total cash flow is identical.

This is structural sequencing. It determines tolerance without changing magnitude.

Financial stress often feels psychological, but it is frequently architectural. When inflow and outflow are tightly synchronized, the system leaves no slack for variance. Slack is not waste. Slack is tolerance.

Sequence sensitivity becomes more pronounced when income is irregular. A professional earning commission-based income may have high annual earnings but variable monthly distribution. If obligations are configured as if income were smooth, instability emerges not from insufficient income but from mismatched assumptions.

Here the distinction between reliable and projected income becomes critical. Reliable income is income that arrives on predictable timing and in predictable magnitude within narrow variance bands. Projected income is income expected based on historical averages but subject to timing or magnitude fluctuation.

Treating projected income as reliable income is a structural error. It compresses tolerance. If obligations are calibrated to projected averages rather than reliable floors, the system becomes dependent on expectation fulfillment.

In stable architecture, obligations are anchored to reliable inflow, not projected upside. Projected income can enhance surplus. It cannot support rigidity.

This distinction is not about pessimism. It is about structural realism. When projected income fails to materialize in a given cycle, the system must compensate. If no buffer exists between reliable inflow and obligation sequencing, compensation takes the form of stress, delay, or credit dependency.

Obligation rigidity compounds this effect. Some obligations are flexible in timing or magnitude. Others are not. Housing payments, insurance premiums, and contractual minimums are rigid. They do not adapt to income variance. They assume payment in full, on schedule.

When rigid obligations consume a high proportion of reliable income, the system's tolerance narrows. Minor variance in inflow now threatens core commitments. The system is not unstable because obligations exist; it is unstable because rigid obligations are calibrated too tightly to expected inflow.

Margin calibration begins here, conceptually. Margin is the gap between reliable inflow and rigid obligation load. It is not yet about optimization or reduction strategies. It is about recognizing that structural gap size determines tolerance.

If reliable monthly income is $6,000 and rigid obligations total $5,800, the structure has minimal calibration margin. A temporary $500 variance produces immediate constraint. If rigid obligations total $4,500, the same variance is absorbed without systemic strain.

Income magnitude has not changed. Configuration has.

Configuration is the determinant of tolerance because it governs how the system behaves under deviation. A system designed only for perfect conditions is fragile. A system designed with variance accommodation maintains continuity under stress.

Tolerance is not comfort. It is survivability without cascade effects.

Cascade effects occur when one deviation triggers secondary consequences. A delayed payment triggers fees. Fees reduce liquidity. Reduced liquidity triggers additional borrowing or delayed payments. Each step compounds the original variance. The structure amplifies disturbance.

In a tolerant configuration, deviation is isolated. A delayed inflow does not automatically disrupt multiple obligations. Spacing, sequencing, and margin absorb the disturbance. The system flexes rather than fractures.

The architectural mindset requires modeling stable conditions and variance conditions simultaneously. Under stable conditions, nearly any configuration appears functional. Under variance conditions, only certain configurations remain coherent.

When evaluating financial structure, the relevant question is not, "Does this work when everything goes right?" The relevant question is, "How does this behave when something is slightly off?"

Small deviations are the norm, not the exception. Payroll shifts. Expenses advance. Income arrives later than expected. Minor medical or travel costs arise. Stability is the capacity to integrate these deviations without structural degradation.

This reframes financial control. Control is not the absence of fluctuation. It is the ability to absorb fluctuation without altering core commitments.

High earners frequently mistake magnitude for immunity. Large incomes mask structural weaknesses because surplus can temporarily compensate for poor configuration. But if rigid obligations scale proportionally with income, the margin does not expand. The system remains tightly coupled at a higher level.

A professional earning $250,000 with rigid obligations calibrated to $235,000 annually has no more tolerance than a professional earning $75,000 with $70,000 in rigid obligations. Both systems operate near structural constraint. Both depend on income continuity. Both are sequence sensitive.

Conversely, a moderate earner who calibrates rigid obligations conservatively relative to reliable inflow can operate with greater structural control than a higher earner who does not.

This is not an argument for minimalism. It is an argument for configuration awareness.

Every financial system has a tolerance threshold. That threshold is defined by how much deviation it can absorb before obligations are disrupted. Configuration determines that threshold.

When inflows are spaced relative to obligations, when rigid commitments are calibrated to reliable income rather than projected peaks, and when sequencing density is moderated, the system gains tolerance.

When inflows and obligations are tightly synchronized, calibrated to expectation, and rigidly clustered, the system loses tolerance.

The architecture either amplifies variance or absorbs it.

Financial control begins not with earning more but with examining configuration. Income magnitude increases potential. Structural configuration determines whether that potential translates into stability.

Control, therefore, is architectural. It is embedded in the design of flows, commitments, and sequencing. The professional who understands this distinction stops chasing magnitude as the sole lever and begins adjusting configuration as the primary determinant of durability.

The remainder of this book builds from that foundation.

PART 1 (continued)

Once configuration becomes the focal variable, a different set of questions emerges. Not "How much do I make?" but "How is my system arranged?" Not "Can I cover my expenses?" but "How does my structure behave when timing shifts?"

Most professionals intuitively assess financial health by surplus at month end. If there is money left over, the system appears functional. But end-of-cycle surplus is a lagging indicator. It does not reveal mid-cycle compression, sequence exposure, or tolerance thresholds. A structure can close each month positive and still operate under continuous strain because its obligations are front-loaded and its inflows are tightly coupled.

This is why financial stress often persists even when arithmetic suggests adequacy. The instability is not mathematical. It is temporal.

Time is the invisible axis of financial architecture. Income is not a lump sum; it is a series of arrivals. Obligations are not abstract totals; they are scheduled extractions. When these two are misaligned in sequence, liquidity fluctuates sharply within the cycle. The sharper the fluctuation, the greater the sensitivity.

Imagine a system in which 70 percent of monthly obligations are due within the first five days. The professional is paid twice monthly, on the

1st and 15th. Under ideal timing, the first paycheck covers the early cluster. The second paycheck covers the remainder. The system appears balanced.

Now introduce minor variance. The first paycheck arrives on the 2nd due to a processing delay. Auto-drafts initiate on the 1st. Temporary overdraft protection engages. Fees apply. The second paycheck must now repair both the remaining obligations and the prior distortion. The structure has not failed because of insufficient annual income. It has failed because sequencing assumed perfect alignment.

Sequence sensitivity increases when the ratio between rigid obligations and reliable inflow tightens. The closer obligations sit to the inflow ceiling, the less time exists between liquidity sufficiency and insufficiency. A narrow band means small variance crosses the threshold quickly.

In contrast, when rigid obligations consume a lower proportion of reliable income, the system gains elasticity. Elasticity is not excess consumption capacity. It is structural breathing room. It allows obligations to be met even when inflow shifts slightly in timing or magnitude.

Elastic systems behave differently under stress. A late inflow does not immediately threaten core commitments. A temporary income dip does not force restructuring within days. The system absorbs and recalibrates over time rather than reacting instantly.

This distinction becomes more pronounced when income composition is mixed. Many professionals operate with a base salary supplemented by variable compensation—bonuses, commissions, project fees, or performance incentives. The structural error occurs when total lifestyle obligations are calibrated to the blended average rather than to the reliable base.

If base salary is \$90,000 and average annual compensation rises to \$120,000 with bonuses, the temptation is to construct obligations at a level that assumes the full \$120,000. In strong years, the system functions.

In weaker cycles, the structure compresses immediately because rigid commitments were anchored to projection rather than reliability.

The disciplined configuration anchors rigidity to the reliable base. Variable income becomes surplus, not structural support. This preserves tolerance across cycles without requiring prediction accuracy.

Prediction error is inevitable. Even in stable industries, compensation structures evolve. Economic conditions shift. Employers restructure. Clients delay payment. A configuration that depends on consistent projection accuracy is inherently fragile.

Reliability, therefore, is not about optimism or pessimism. It is about defining the minimum dependable inflow band and calibrating structural commitments within that band.

Obligation rigidity amplifies this dynamic. Not all expenses exert equal structural force. Variable consumption—dining, discretionary travel, flexible subscriptions—can be reduced with relative ease. Rigid obligations—housing contracts, long-term leases, installment agreements—cannot adjust quickly. Their timelines and magnitudes are externally defined.

When rigid commitments dominate the expense profile, the system becomes less adaptable. Flexibility exists only at the margins. If those margins are thin, adaptability is illusory.

This is why configuration, not total expense, determines tolerance. Two professionals may both spend $8,000 per month. One may allocate $5,000 to rigid commitments and $3,000 to flexible categories. The other may commit $7,500 to rigid obligations and retain only $500 as adjustable spending. Under stable conditions, both appear equivalent. Under variance, their behaviors diverge dramatically.

In the first configuration, income disruption can be absorbed by temporary contraction of flexible categories without threatening core stability. In the second, even minor disruption threatens structural commitments because flexibility is insufficient to compensate.

This is margin calibration in its introductory form. It is the intentional spacing between reliable inflow and rigid obligation load. Calibration is not about austerity. It is about determining how much deviation the system can tolerate before core commitments are at risk.

Calibration interacts directly with timing coupling. Even with adequate margin in aggregate terms, poor sequencing can create temporary compression. If large rigid obligations cluster before sufficient inflow accumulates, the system experiences periodic stress despite annual adequacy.

Over time, repeated compression erodes perceived control. Even if the system mathematically survives, the experience is one of fragility. Financial control is not merely solvency. It is structural predictability under variance.

Predictability arises when configuration reduces sensitivity to small disruptions. Reduced sensitivity is achieved by widening the gap between reliable inflow and rigid obligations, spacing obligations across the cycle, and preventing projected income from underwriting fixed commitments.

As income rises, complexity often increases. More subscriptions, larger housing costs, additional financing arrangements, higher insurance premiums. Without deliberate calibration, obligation rigidity scales alongside income magnitude. The system expands but does not strengthen. It becomes a larger version of the same fragile structure.

Durable systems scale differently. As income increases, reliable inflow floors are reassessed. Rigid commitments are expanded cautiously relative to that floor. Variable income remains variable in structural treatment. Timing coupling is monitored. Sequencing density is managed.

The result is not necessarily minimal expenditure. It is proportional rigidity.

Proportional rigidity determines how the system behaves when external conditions shift. In stable economic periods, high rigidity may feel efficient. In unstable periods, it becomes restrictive. The same structure that felt optimized under growth becomes compressed under contraction.

Configuration determines whether contraction is manageable or destabilizing.

Financial control, then, is not achieved through motivational intensity or income pursuit alone. It is achieved through structural awareness and deliberate calibration. A professional who understands their configuration can model how the system responds to delayed income, temporary reduction, or clustered obligations. They can identify where sensitivity is concentrated.

Where sensitivity concentrates, tolerance is lowest.

This is the architectural lens: identify concentration of rigidity, clustering of timing, dependence on projection, and narrow margin between reliable inflow and obligation load. These variables interact. When they align poorly, minor variance cascades. When aligned deliberately, variance is absorbed.

Income magnitude provides capacity. Configuration determines resilience.

Configuration is not static. It evolves as income sources change, as obligations accumulate, and as life complexity increases. The structural error most professionals make is allowing configuration to evolve reactively. Income rises and commitments expand in response. A new obligation is added because current inflow appears sufficient. A larger fixed cost is accepted because projected compensation supports it. Each decision is individually rational. Collectively, they alter system tolerance.

Over time, rigidity density increases without explicit recalibration of reliability assumptions.

Rigidity density refers to the proportion of total financial capacity that is contractually fixed and time-bound. As rigidity density rises, optionality declines. Optionality is not luxury spending. It is the structural ability to reallocate, delay, or reduce outflow without breaching commitments. When optionality declines, the system's response to variance narrows.

Consider a professional whose reliable income supports $4,000 of rigid monthly commitments. Over several years, income increases and lifestyle expands. Housing is upgraded. Vehicle financing is added. Long-term service contracts accumulate. Rigid commitments rise to $7,500. Income also rises, but the reliable floor has not expanded proportionally. Variable compensation represents a growing share of total earnings.

Under expansionary conditions, the system feels stronger. Total earnings are higher. Surplus appears larger in strong months. Yet rigidity density has increased relative to the reliable base. The system now depends more heavily on projected income to sustain fixed commitments.

When projected income underperforms—even temporarily—the structural gap closes quickly. What felt like growth reveals itself as increased coupling to variability.

This is how high earners experience instability without income collapse. The issue is not magnitude. It is calibration relative to reliability.

Sequence sensitivity compounds as systems grow more complex. More obligations mean more dates, more auto-drafts, more coordination between inflow and outflow. Each additional rigid commitment introduces another timing node. The more nodes, the more potential points of misalignment.

In small systems, timing misalignment may affect one or two obligations. In complex systems, it may cascade across many. Structural simplicity enhances tolerance not because it reduces ambition, but because it reduces coupling density.

Coupling density is the degree to which multiple obligations depend on precise inflow timing. When five rigid commitments are due within three days of a paycheck, coupling density is high. When those same commitments are distributed across the cycle, density decreases. The total obligation load is unchanged. The structural behavior is not.

Distributed sequencing reduces the probability that a single inflow variance disrupts multiple commitments simultaneously. It isolates variance. Isolation prevents cascade.

Financial control, at this foundational level, is about isolating variance rather than eliminating it. Variance is inherent in economic life. Income timing shifts. Expense timing shifts. Markets change. Employers restructure. Clients delay payment. Structural configuration determines whether these shifts remain localized disturbances or expand into systemic stress.

Tolerance, therefore, is a function of spacing, proportional rigidity, and reliability anchoring.

Spacing refers to the distribution of obligations relative to inflow timing. Proportional rigidity refers to how much of reliable inflow is committed to non-adjustable obligations. Reliability anchoring refers to calibrating commitments to dependable income floors rather than projected peaks.

When these three are aligned, the system exhibits controlled behavior under deviation. When misaligned, even small shocks produce outsized consequences.

Over extended time horizons, configuration choices compound. A tightly calibrated system may function for years under favorable conditions. Because no major disruption occurs, fragility remains hidden. This creates a false sense of robustness. Structural weaknesses are only revealed when conditions deviate.

Durable architecture assumes deviation as normal. It does not optimize for best-case scenarios. It designs for continuity under mild-to-moderate stress.

This orientation alters decision-making. A housing upgrade is evaluated not only for affordability at current income, but for sustainability at the reliable floor. A new fixed commitment is assessed not only for monthly cost, but for its effect on rigidity density and sequence coupling. Variable income is treated as enhancement, not foundation.

The professional who internalizes this framework stops asking whether they can afford something in the present month. They ask whether the commitment preserves tolerance under variance.

Tolerance is the core asset. Without tolerance, every fluctuation demands reaction. With tolerance, fluctuations are integrated without destabilizing the system.

This distinction reframes financial control from reactive management to structural design. Reactive systems rely on constant attention. They require monitoring balances daily, adjusting transfers, negotiating due dates, and compensating for misalignment. Structural systems require design discipline upfront but less continuous correction.

Control is not about micromanaging every dollar. It is about constructing a configuration that does not require constant intervention to remain coherent.

As this framework develops in subsequent chapters, margin compression, liquidity runway, and exposure stacking will be analyzed in detail. For now, the essential foundation is clear: income magnitude is secondary to configuration. Timing coupling amplifies minor variance. Sequence sensitivity reveals fragility. Reliable income anchors commitments. Obligation rigidity must be calibrated deliberately. Configuration determines tolerance.

Financial stability is architectural.

At a deeper level, configuration determines not only whether obligations can be met, but how decisions are made under pressure. When tolerance is narrow, decision-making becomes short-horizon. Choices are optimized for immediate relief rather than long-term coherence. This behavioral shift is not a failure of discipline. It is a predictable consequence of structural compression.

In tightly configured systems, minor disruptions force immediate tradeoffs. Which payment is delayed. Which expense is deferred. Which transfer is canceled. Each adjustment is tactical. Over time, repeated tactical adjustments create structural drift. Accounts are repurposed. Informal borrowing between categories becomes routine. Timing workarounds substitute for architectural correction.

The system continues operating, but control deteriorates.

When configuration is tolerant, decision-making expands in horizon. A temporary income dip does not require immediate structural compromise. The professional can assess, reallocate, and adjust deliberately rather than defensively. The presence of tolerance preserves strategic capacity.

This is an underappreciated dimension of financial architecture: configuration governs cognitive load. High coupling and narrow margin demand constant monitoring. Low coupling and calibrated rigidity reduce surveillance requirements. The system sustains itself with less intervention.

Cognitive load is not abstract. It affects professional performance, negotiation confidence, and risk assessment. A system that is always near constraint amplifies perceived risk. Even opportunities with positive long-term asymmetry may be rejected because short-term compression cannot be absorbed.

Thus configuration shapes optionality.

Optionality is the structural ability to make choices without destabilizing commitments. It is not excess consumption. It is the freedom to change employers, reduce workload temporarily, pursue additional training, or decline unfavorable contracts without triggering immediate financial strain.

Optionality expands when reliable inflow exceeds rigid commitments by a meaningful margin and when sequencing does not cluster obligations tightly around single inflow events. Optionality contracts when projected income supports fixed commitments and when timing coupling leaves no buffer for delay.

Over extended periods, optionality influences career trajectory. Professionals operating within tolerant systems can accept roles with variable upside, endure transitional income phases, or withstand short-term volatility because their architecture absorbs fluctuation. Those operating within tightly coupled systems must prioritize income stability above all else, even when stability comes at the expense of long-term growth or autonomy.

Configuration therefore affects not only present stability but future strategic positioning.

Exposure concentration is another structural dimension that interacts with configuration, even at this introductory stage. When income is derived from a single source and obligations are calibrated tightly to that source, exposure is concentrated. If that source weakens, the entire system is stressed simultaneously. If obligations are diversified in timing and calibrated conservatively relative to reliable inflow, concentration risk is moderated.

The purpose here is not to eliminate concentration entirely—many careers inherently involve concentrated income streams. The purpose is to recognize how configuration either amplifies or dampens that concentration. A single income source with low rigidity density is structurally different from a single income source with high rigidity density.

In both cases, magnitude may be identical. Tolerance differs.

Configuration also governs recovery velocity. When a variance event occurs—temporary income reduction, unexpected expense, timing delay—the speed at which the system returns to baseline depends on margin calibration and sequencing flexibility. Systems with narrow gaps and high rigidity recover slowly because each cycle remains near constraint. Systems with wider calibration gaps can re-stabilize within fewer cycles.

Recovery velocity matters because instability rarely occurs as a single isolated event. Variance tends to cluster across time. A delayed payment may coincide with a seasonal expense increase. A compensation adjustment may align with an insurance renewal. If the first deviation consumes available margin, the second encounters a weakened structure.

Durable architecture anticipates clustering as normal rather than exceptional. It preserves enough tolerance so that sequential minor disruptions do not accumulate into structural stress.

This is the core shift from reactive budgeting to architectural design. Budgeting tracks categories and totals. Architecture models behavior under variance.

In a budget-centric mindset, the question is whether monthly expenses equal monthly income. In an architectural mindset, the question is how obligations interact with inflow timing, how much of reliable income is locked into rigidity, and how the system behaves when expectations are not met precisely.

The difference appears subtle but is foundational. Budgets manage flows within a given structure. Architecture defines the structure itself.

Professionals who operate without architectural awareness often experience a recurring pattern: income rises, obligations expand, stress remains constant. The absolute numbers change. The tolerance threshold does not. Because configuration was not addressed, magnitude increases simply rescale the existing fragility.

Conversely, when configuration is addressed first, magnitude increases can strengthen the system rather than merely enlarge it. Additional income can expand calibration margin, reduce rigidity proportionally, and improve sequencing flexibility instead of funding new fixed commitments.

This requires deliberate constraint. Not moral constraint, but structural discipline. Each new rigid obligation must be evaluated relative to reliable inflow and existing rigidity density. Each timing cluster must be examined for coupling risk. Each assumption about projected income must be treated as contingent.

Financial control is therefore less about optimism or pessimism and more about design realism. Systems designed with narrow tolerance depend on favorable conditions. Systems designed with calibrated tolerance remain coherent across a wider range of conditions.

Configuration is the determinant of that range.

As the analysis deepens in subsequent chapters, the mechanisms that compress margin, extend liquidity, and manage exposure will be examined in isolation and interaction. For now, the central principle stands without qualification: financial stability is not a function of how much enters the system. It is a function of how the system is built.

The architecture precedes the arithmetic.

There is a final structural distinction that must be established before moving beyond this foundation: stability is not a static state. It is a range of conditions within which the system remains coherent.

Most professionals evaluate stability as binary. Bills are paid or not paid. Accounts are positive or negative. Commitments are honored or breached. But architectural stability is gradient-based. A system can be technically solvent yet structurally fragile. It can meet obligations while operating at the edge of tolerance. It can appear stable while being highly sensitive to small disturbances.

The determinant of stability is the width of the operational range between reliable inflow and rigid commitment.

If reliable monthly inflow is narrowly above rigid obligation load, the operational range is thin. The system remains coherent only within a tight variance band. A small timing delay or moderate expense fluctuation pushes it toward constraint. It may not collapse, but it must compensate immediately.

If reliable inflow exceeds rigid commitments by a wider structural gap, the operational range expands. The system remains coherent across a broader set of conditions. It can absorb not only timing shifts but moderate magnitude variance without reconfiguration.

This range defines tolerance.

Tolerance is measurable not by surplus alone, but by the distance between structural commitments and dependable income floors. It is also shaped by sequencing density and obligation clustering. A wide aggregate gap can still produce temporary instability if timing coupling compresses liquidity at specific intervals. Thus tolerance must be evaluated across time, not only in aggregate.

Time-distributed tolerance is stronger than point-in-time tolerance.

A system that survives only because inflow and outflow align perfectly at specific moments is structurally brittle. A system that remains coherent across multiple points in the cycle—even when inflow shifts modestly—is structurally resilient.

This difference becomes especially significant during transitional periods. Career changes, geographic relocation, family expansion, entrepreneurial experimentation, or industry contraction all introduce temporary variance. The professional who has designed for narrow operational range must delay or avoid transition because the system cannot absorb short-term deviation. The professional with calibrated tolerance can transition without destabilizing core commitments.

Thus configuration determines adaptability.

Adaptability is not constant change. It is the capacity to change without structural fracture.

When rigid obligations dominate reliable inflow and are tightly coupled to timing assumptions, adaptability declines sharply. Even voluntary positive changes—such as pursuing additional education or shifting to a role with deferred compensation—become structurally infeasible. The system has no slack to accommodate interim adjustment.

Slack, in this context, is not inefficiency. It is structural reserve. It creates space for decision-making without cascade.

Cascade remains the central risk in fragile architectures. One late inflow triggers a missed obligation. The missed obligation triggers penalties or interest. Liquidity is further reduced. Additional obligations become stressed. The system enters a feedback loop. What began as minor variance becomes compounded instability.

Cascade is rarely dramatic at first. It begins with small distortions. But without margin and sequencing flexibility, distortions accumulate.

In tolerant architectures, distortions dissipate. A late inflow may delay discretionary spending but does not jeopardize rigid commitments. A temporary expense spike may reduce surplus accumulation but does not force borrowing or obligation deferral. The disturbance is absorbed and the system returns to baseline within one or two cycles.

Return-to-baseline speed is an indicator of architectural strength. The faster a system re-stabilizes after deviation, the wider its tolerance band.

This is why financial control cannot be evaluated solely by income level or net worth snapshots. A high-income professional with high rigidity density and tight coupling may require months to recover from minor disruption. A moderate-income professional with calibrated commitments and distributed sequencing may recover within a single cycle.

Configuration governs recovery dynamics.

Over long horizons, systems that recover quickly accumulate resilience. Systems that recover slowly accumulate stress. Slow recovery compresses future tolerance because each disturbance weakens the structure incrementally. Fees, short-term borrowing, and deferred adjustments erode margin. Over time, fragility deepens even if income remains constant.

Durable financial control requires designing for non-catastrophic variance. It assumes that minor disruption will occur regularly. It assumes that projection error is normal. It assumes that timing will not always align perfectly. It embeds these assumptions into the configuration itself.

The central claim of this chapter is therefore architectural rather than motivational: stability is engineered through configuration. Income magnitude provides potential energy. Configuration determines whether that energy is stored as resilience or dissipated through fragility.

When reliable inflow anchors rigid commitments conservatively, when obligations are sequenced to avoid clustering, when projected income does not underwrite fixed commitments, and when proportional rigidity is monitored as income scales, the system gains tolerance. When these elements are ignored, magnitude alone cannot prevent instability.

Financial control begins at the level of design.

The architecture either narrows the range of survivable conditions or widens it. Everything that follows in this book builds upon that single distinction.

If financial control is architectural, then instability is rarely accidental. It is embedded in design choices that were never evaluated as design choices. Most obligations are accepted individually. A housing contract is signed because it is affordable in the present month. A vehicle is financed because the payment fits current cash flow. A subscription is added because the incremental cost appears negligible. Each decision is locally rational.

Architecture, however, is global.

Every additional rigid obligation narrows the operational range unless reliable inflow expands proportionally. Every timing cluster increases coupling density unless sequencing is intentionally redistributed. Every assumption that projected income will persist converts variability into structural dependency.

Because these shifts occur incrementally, fragility often emerges gradually. There is no single moment of collapse. Instead, there is progressive tightening. Liquidity feels thinner at the end of each cycle. Flexibility diminishes. Decision-making shortens in horizon. The professional works harder to maintain the same level of stability.

This progressive tightening is often misdiagnosed as insufficient income. Income increases are pursued as the primary remedy. Yet if configuration is not addressed, new income simply fills newly expanded commitments. Rigidity density remains constant. Tolerance does not widen.

The system scales without strengthening.

Strengthening requires deliberate asymmetry: reliable inflow must grow faster than rigid commitment, or rigid commitment must grow more slowly than inflow. Without that asymmetry, structural capacity remains flat.

This principle applies across income bands. Early-career professionals face low magnitude but often maintain lower rigidity density, which provides hidden tolerance. Mid-career professionals frequently experience the opposite. Income increases, but commitments expand in parallel—larger housing costs, educational obligations, financed consumption, contractual services. The apparent improvement in capacity masks unchanged structural tightness.

Late-career professionals may then encounter reduced income variability tolerance if compensation shifts toward performance-based incentives or if employment concentration increases. If rigidity was calibrated during peak earnings, the system becomes sensitive precisely when income reliability narrows.

These lifecycle transitions reveal whether configuration was conservative or optimistic.

Conservative configuration does not imply minimal ambition. It implies anchoring structural commitments to the most dependable income layer. It implies treating upside as enhancement rather than entitlement. It implies evaluating obligation additions not only for present affordability but for variance survivability.

Variance survivability is the ability of the system to withstand non-catastrophic income reduction or timing shift without breaching rigid commitments.

Breaching rigid commitments introduces external control into the system. Late fees, interest penalties, credit restrictions, contractual consequences—these are forms of structural coercion. When commitments cannot be met as scheduled, optionality contracts sharply because external constraints dictate behavior.

Thus architectural fragility eventually becomes behavioral constraint.

In contrast, when commitments are calibrated below the reliable inflow ceiling, control remains internal. Adjustments can be made without invoking penalty structures. The system remains self-governing.

Self-governance is a defining feature of financial control.

This distinction also reframes the concept of affordability. Affordability is commonly assessed as whether payment fits within current monthly income. Architectural affordability asks a different question: does this commitment preserve tolerance under variance? Does it increase coupling density? Does it raise rigidity proportion beyond reliable anchoring?

A commitment can be affordable in the narrow sense and destabilizing in the structural sense.

For example, a professional receiving a large annual bonus may use that bonus to justify a higher recurring fixed expense. The arithmetic appears sound when averaged across twelve months. Yet the recurring expense is rigid and time-bound, while the bonus is projected and contingent. The structure now assumes bonus continuity. If a single year underperforms, rigidity remains constant while inflow declines.

What was treated as surplus becomes embedded into structural baseline.

This embedding process is central to instability. Surplus that becomes commitment reduces tolerance. Surplus that remains variable preserves tolerance.

Over time, the difference compounds. Systems that consistently embed surplus into rigidity become increasingly dependent on growth to remain stable. Systems that preserve surplus as flexible capacity accumulate widening tolerance.

Growth-dependent stability is fragile because it requires continued favorable conditions. Tolerance-based stability is durable because it assumes variability.

This architectural framing also clarifies the relationship between control and freedom. Control is not the elimination of obligation. It is the proportional alignment of obligation to dependable capacity. When that alignment is maintained, obligations can expand without eliminating tolerance. When alignment is ignored, obligation expansion erodes freedom even as income rises.

Freedom, in this structural sense, is not discretionary spending power. It is the absence of forced reaction under minor stress.

A financially controlled system does not panic when inflow shifts slightly. It does not require immediate renegotiation of commitments. It does not depend on precision timing to remain solvent. It maintains coherence across a reasonable range of conditions.

Configuration determines that coherence.

The architecture of financial control therefore begins with a disciplined recognition: income magnitude is potential energy. Without structural calibration, that energy dissipates into rigidity and coupling. With structural calibration, that energy builds tolerance and optionality.

The professional who understands this distinction stops pursuing stability solely through income expansion and begins engineering stability through configuration.

From this point forward, every structural concept introduced—margin compression, liquidity runway, exposure stacking, obligation rigidity—will build upon this architecture. But none of those mechanisms can compensate for a misconfigured foundation.

Stability is not purchased. It is designed.

Architectural clarity changes how financial data is interpreted. Instead of asking whether current cash flow is positive, the question becomes whether the system is positioned to remain coherent when conditions shift. Instead of focusing on aggregate totals, attention shifts to structural relationships: dependable inflow relative to rigid obligation load, obligation sequencing relative to inflow timing, and projected income relative to fixed commitments.

These relationships determine the system's behavior.

Behavior under ideal conditions is largely irrelevant. Nearly any configuration can function when inflow arrives on time, projected income materializes, and expenses remain predictable. The relevant test is deviation within ordinary bounds. A late payroll cycle. A smaller-than-expected bonus. A temporary client delay. A clustered expense month. These are not rare anomalies. They are normal features of economic life.

A system designed only for precision will experience normal variation as crisis. A system designed with tolerance will experience normal variation as noise.

This distinction explains why two professionals with identical income can experience entirely different subjective realities. One lives in continuous vigilance, monitoring balances, anticipating due dates, and adjusting transfers to avoid friction. The other operates with structural slack, knowing that minor timing shifts do not threaten core commitments. The arithmetic may be similar. The architecture is not.

Architecture governs stress distribution.

When rigid commitments are tightly aligned with reliable inflow and clustered around narrow timing windows, stress concentrates. When commitments are calibrated below reliable inflow and distributed across time, stress disperses. Dispersed stress is manageable. Concentrated stress feels acute even if total obligation load is unchanged.

The system's design either amplifies or diffuses pressure.

This amplification dynamic becomes especially important as complexity increases. More accounts, more obligations, and more income sources create more potential interaction points. Without deliberate configuration, interaction points multiply sensitivity. With deliberate configuration, interaction points can be structured to isolate risk.

Isolation is foundational. If a single inflow delay jeopardizes multiple rigid commitments, isolation is absent. If that same delay affects only surplus allocation while core commitments remain secure, isolation is present.

Isolation is achieved through calibration and sequencing discipline. Calibration ensures rigid commitments remain anchored below reliable inflow thresholds. Sequencing ensures obligations are not overly concentrated around single inflow events. Together, they widen the operational range of the system.

Operational range is the true measure of financial control. It defines how far conditions can move before structural reconfiguration is required.

A narrow operational range produces reactive behavior. A wide operational range produces measured adjustment. Over long horizons, this difference compounds. Reactive systems expend energy maintaining stability. Measured systems preserve energy for advancement.

Advancement requires optionality. Optionality requires tolerance. Tolerance requires configuration.

This chain is not motivational; it is structural. When tolerance is present, professionals can absorb moderate uncertainty in exchange for strategic opportunity. When tolerance is absent, certainty becomes mandatory because any deviation threatens core commitments. As a result, tightly configured systems bias toward short-term income security even when long-term positioning suffers.

Configuration therefore influences career mobility, negotiation leverage, and risk acceptance. It determines whether income must remain stable at all costs or whether moderate fluctuation can be integrated without destabilization.

The architectural perspective also clarifies that stability does not require extreme conservatism. It requires proportional alignment. A high-income professional can maintain substantial commitments and still preserve tolerance if those commitments remain meaningfully below reliable inflow and are sequenced intelligently. Conversely, a moderate-income professional can eliminate tolerance entirely by calibrating rigid obligations at the edge of dependable capacity.

Magnitude does not guarantee safety. Configuration defines it.

As this book progresses, each structural mechanism will be examined with greater precision. Margin compression will explain how operational range narrows invisibly. Liquidity runway will define how long the system can remain coherent under sustained deviation. Exposure stacking will clarify how correlated risks amplify instability. Obligation rigidity will be dissected in depth.

But none of those mechanisms alter the central premise established here.

Financial stability is not the result of earning more alone. It is the result of designing a system in which reliable inflow, obligation rigidity, and timing sequencing interact within a tolerable range. It is the product of architectural decisions made deliberately rather than incrementally.

Income magnitude determines how large the system can become. Structural configuration determines how stable it remains as it grows.

The architecture comes first.

Reliable Income vs Projected Income

Income volatility bands are not theoretical constructs. They are observable patterns across time. Yet most professionals do not examine them formally. They experience income as a sequence of deposits, not as a distribution with measurable dispersion.

A distribution has a center and a spread. The center is often mistaken for stability. The spread determines reliability.

If income over a five-year period fluctuates between $110,000 and $170,000, the average may sit near $140,000. The psychological anchor becomes $140,000. Yet the volatility band spans $60,000. That spread defines structural risk. The lower bound, not the mean, defines dependable capacity.

The relevant question is not what income has averaged, but how frequently it has approached the lower end of its band and under what conditions. If the lower bound appears during mild economic contraction, industry shifts, or performance variance, then it must be treated as structurally plausible in the future.

Reliable income floor, therefore, is a probabilistic floor. It reflects what can be expected across normal fluctuations, not exceptional downturns but not exceptional peaks either. It is derived from observing how income behaves when conditions are merely less favorable, not catastrophic.

In stable employment structures, the volatility band may be narrow enough that the reliable floor approximates current income. In performance-based structures, the band may be wide enough that the reliable floor is materially lower than recent realized income.

Defining the reliable floor requires disaggregation. Base compensation must be separated from incentives. Recurring client revenue must be separated from opportunistic projects. Contractual renewals must be distinguished from discretionary bonuses. Each income component has its own volatility band.

Blending components obscures risk.

When all income streams are averaged together, the composite figure masks variability. Architectural clarity requires isolating the narrowest bands from the widest and assigning structural weight accordingly. Narrow bands support rigidity. Wide bands support optionality only if preserved as variable capacity.

Projection drift accelerates when volatility is temporarily suppressed. In prolonged economic expansion, incentive compensation may stabilize at elevated levels. Businesses may experience steady growth across multiple cycles. Commission structures may produce consistent highs. The volatility band appears to compress.

Yet compression of observed variance does not eliminate underlying exposure. It may simply reflect favorable conditions. When commitments expand in response to this apparent stability, the system becomes dependent on the continuation of those conditions.

When variance re-emerges, the adjustment is abrupt because commitments were built on suppressed volatility assumptions.

This is why prosperity often plants the seeds of future instability. Not because prosperity is harmful, but because it encourages structural embedding of surplus.

Embedding surplus converts conditional income into fixed cost support. Once embedded, reversal requires either income recovery or commitment reduction. If reduction is slow or constrained, compression persists.

Asymmetry must therefore be preserved deliberately. Upside should widen margin, not widen rigidity. Downside should narrow surplus, not threaten commitments.

This asymmetry creates structural shock absorption. In a system anchored to reliable floors, positive variance increases optional capacity—additional savings, investment, discretionary allocation. Negative variance reduces that optional capacity but does not immediately disrupt core commitments.

In a system anchored to projection, positive variance merely maintains equilibrium, while negative variance forces correction. The system has no buffer because projection has been normalized into baseline.

Over extended time horizons, the difference between these two orientations is profound. The first accumulates optionality across cycles because surplus is not consumed by rigidity expansion. The second oscillates between expansion during prosperity and contraction during variance, often eroding net capacity over time.

Repeated miscalibration carries cumulative structural consequences.

Each time projected income is treated as reliable and commitments are expanded accordingly, the system becomes more sensitive to volatility. Sensitivity compounds because commitments are typically long-term. A housing upgrade may last decades. Financing agreements span years. Contractual services auto-renew.

If income reverts toward its reliable floor while commitments remain at projected levels, compression becomes chronic rather than episodic. Chronic compression reduces flexibility in other domains. Professional mobility decreases because stable income becomes mandatory. Risk-taking capacity declines because downside variance is no longer tolerable.

Over time, the system's strategic posture narrows.

In some cases, professionals attempt to solve miscalibration by pursuing additional income streams to re-establish projection levels. This can temporarily restore equilibrium. Yet if new income sources are also variable, the volatility band may widen further. Without recalibration of rigidity to dependable floors, the structural problem remains.

Reliability must therefore be defined before expansion.

Reliability as a design principle requires that structural commitments be justified against statistically defensible income baselines. It rejects recent prosperity as sufficient evidence of permanence. It treats upside as provisional until sustained across multiple cycles with demonstrable reduction in volatility.

This orientation is neither conservative nor aggressive. It is structural.

Professionals who adopt reliability as a design principle often discover that their perceived income is less dependable than assumed. The adjustment may require restraint in commitment expansion. Yet this restraint produces long-term stability rather than cyclical contraction.

Reliability also clarifies strategic allocation of surplus. When upside is recognized as conditional, it can be directed toward strengthening the system rather than expanding rigidity. The result is widening tolerance across time rather than increased exposure to variance.

A system built on reliable floors is not immune to economic change. It remains exposed to severe shocks. But it is structurally aligned with ordinary volatility. It does not treat common fluctuation as anomaly.

Income magnitude remains important. Yet without classification into reliable and projected components, magnitude obscures risk. Stability depends on recognizing that not all dollars carry equal structural weight.

Reliable dollars support commitments. Projected dollars support flexibility.

Confusing the two narrows tolerance invisibly. Distinguishing them preserves structural integrity across cycles.

The reliable income floor is not fixed permanently. It evolves, but only when volatility demonstrably narrows across sustained periods and across varied conditions. An increase in base salary shifts the floor immediately because its variance band is narrow. A sequence of strong commission years does not necessarily shift the floor unless the underlying structure of compensation has changed in a way that reduces variability.

This distinction prevents premature recalibration.

Premature recalibration occurs when professionals interpret temporary elevation as structural change. A business owner experiences two exceptional years and assumes revenue has permanently reset to a higher plateau. A senior employee receives several large discretionary bonuses and internalizes them as ongoing compensation. Commitments expand in response. If the elevation proves cyclical rather than structural, compression follows.

Structural change must be distinguished from cyclical fluctuation.

Structural change narrows volatility bands durably. For example, if a professional transitions from commission-heavy compensation to a higher fixed salary with smaller variable components, the reliable floor rises because variance decreases. If a business shifts from opportunistic project work to recurring contractual revenue, the reliable floor may rise even if total income remains similar. The key is not magnitude increase but variance reduction.

Variance reduction increases reliability.

Reliability is therefore not solely about income level. It is about predictability. Two incomes of equal size may have radically different structural roles depending on variance bands.

This becomes especially important in industries subject to macroeconomic cycles. During expansion, volatility appears subdued. During contraction, it widens abruptly. Systems anchored to projected peaks experience rapid compression because commitments were justified under temporarily compressed volatility bands.

Anchoring to reliable floors moderates this effect. When contraction occurs, realized income may decline toward the lower bound, but commitments remain aligned with that bound. Adjustment occurs in surplus rather than in core obligations.

The asymmetry between upside and downside extends beyond immediate compression. Upside variance, when preserved as surplus, compounds capacity. Downside variance, when commitments are misaligned, compounds constraint.

If upside is consistently embedded into rigidity, each expansion phase increases baseline commitment. When contraction arrives, baseline remains elevated while inflow declines. Recovery then requires either income rebound or commitment reduction. If contraction persists, multiple cycles may be required to re-stabilize.

If upside is preserved as flexible capacity, each expansion phase increases resilience rather than obligation. When contraction arrives, resilience absorbs variance. Recovery is faster because baseline commitments were never expanded beyond reliable floors.

Across decades, these small calibration decisions produce divergent trajectories. One trajectory is cyclical and reactive, with alternating expansion and compression. The other is cumulative and stabilizing, with gradual widening of tolerance.

Repeated miscalibration also alters perception of risk.

When professionals experience compression after projection drift, they often attribute instability to external volatility rather than internal configuration. The narrative becomes one of unpredictable markets or unreliable employers. While external factors influence realized income, the structural vulnerability arose from embedding projection into rigidity.

Without recognizing this, the same pattern may repeat. Prosperity returns. Commitments expand again. Contraction follows. The cycle persists.

Reliability as a design principle interrupts this cycle. It demands that commitments be evaluated against dependable baselines rather than aspirational averages. It requires examining multi-year income distributions rather than recent performance.

This does not imply static living standards. It implies that expansion in rigidity should lag sustained reduction in volatility, not precede it.

Lag is protective. It allows time for variance patterns to reveal whether recent income increases are structural or cyclical. It prevents commitment escalation based on incomplete data.

In practice, this means observing income behavior across different conditions before recalibrating the reliable floor upward. If income remains elevated through both favorable and moderately unfavorable environments, the volatility band may have narrowed legitimately. Only then does raising the reliable floor reflect structural change rather than optimism.

This disciplined approach produces slower rigidity expansion but stronger long-term stability.

It also clarifies how to treat irregular but recurring income components. Some professionals receive annual bonuses that are highly probable but not contractually guaranteed. Others have recurring client relationships that historically renew but lack long-term contracts. These components occupy a middle position between reliable and speculative.

Structurally, they must be discounted relative to base salary. The degree of discount depends on observed variance. If renewal rates are near certain across multiple cycles, the reliable floor may include a portion of that income. If renewal rates fluctuate materially, inclusion should be conservative.

The purpose is not to eliminate reasonable expectation. It is to avoid calibrating rigidity to the upper bound of probability.

When commitments are anchored to conservative probability, realized income exceeding that level creates surplus. When commitments are anchored to optimistic probability, realized income below that level creates compression.

Compression is structurally asymmetric. Surplus can be deferred or allocated flexibly. Compression requires action. Action under compression is constrained by time and contract.

Over long horizons, the cumulative effect of anchoring to reliable floors is the preservation of internal control. Professionals remain in position to decide rather than react. Income fluctuations alter surplus accumulation rather than threaten core commitments.

Reliability, then, is not a mood of caution. It is a method of separating statistical consistency from expectation. It is the discipline of building on what is demonstrably stable rather than what is recently favorable.

Financial systems built on expectation alone are vulnerable to variance reversion. Systems built on reliable floors integrate variance as ordinary.

The distinction is subtle in expansionary periods and decisive in contractionary ones.

When volatility inevitably returns to historical ranges, the system reveals whether it was designed for averages or for dependable baselines.

Reliability as a design principle ultimately changes how growth is interpreted.

Growth in income can mean two very different things. It can mean an upward shift in the reliable floor, reflecting reduced volatility and increased predictability. Or it can mean an upward expansion of the volatility band, where higher peaks coexist with persistent lower bounds. Both increase average income. Only one increases dependable capacity.

If average income rises from $140,000 to $180,000 but the lower bound remains near $120,000, the volatility band has widened. The professional is earning more, but dependable capacity has not increased proportionally. If commitments are expanded to match $180,000, the system becomes more sensitive, not less.

If average income rises and the lower bound rises with it—because compensation structure has changed or recurring revenue has become contractual—then the reliable floor shifts upward. Commitments anchored to that new floor remain structurally sound.

The critical variable is not peak income. It is the movement of the lower bound.

This reframing prevents a common misinterpretation: assuming that higher income automatically produces greater stability. Higher income increases potential surplus. Stability increases only when reliable floors rise relative to rigid commitments.

When reliability is ignored, prosperity can conceal fragility. During extended favorable cycles, projected income feels statistically certain because it has been repeatedly realized. The volatility band appears compressed not because underlying variability has disappeared, but because recent history has been uniformly positive.

This produces a subtle distortion. The memory of peak income displaces awareness of lower bounds. Commitments are justified against recent highs rather than against full-cycle distributions. The system begins to depend on continuation of conditions that are, by definition, cyclical.

When those conditions shift—even moderately—the system must adjust quickly. If rigid commitments were calibrated to peaks, adjustment occurs through contraction of surplus, then contraction of flexibility, and eventually contraction of autonomy.

Autonomy is lost when financial decisions are forced by structural misalignment rather than chosen strategically.

Repeated miscalibration also affects behavioral thresholds. If a professional has repeatedly expanded commitments during prosperity and then endured contraction during downturns, they may begin to distrust income variability itself. Instead of recalibrating commitments to reliable floors, they may attempt to eliminate volatility entirely by pursuing roles with absolute income stability, even at the cost of long-term opportunity.

In this way, projection-based calibration can narrow future optionality twice: first through compression during downturns, and later through avoidance of beneficial risk.

Reliability-based calibration avoids both extremes. It allows participation in upside while insulating core commitments from downside. It preserves the ability to absorb volatility without either overextending during peaks or retreating excessively after contractions.

Over decades, this distinction compounds.

A system anchored to projected income tends to oscillate. During expansion, commitments grow. During contraction, they are stressed. Recovery may require years. Each cycle introduces friction—transaction costs, emotional strain, reduced strategic flexibility. Net capacity may stagnate despite high average income because volatility erodes structural integrity.

A system anchored to reliable floors tends to accumulate stability. Surplus during expansion increases resilience rather than obligation. Contraction reduces surplus but not core coherence. Recovery is faster because commitments never exceeded dependable capacity. Net capacity expands steadily even if peak income fluctuates.

This steady accumulation of stability does not attract attention in prosperous periods. It becomes decisive when variance returns.

Reliability, therefore, is not conservative posture for its own sake. It is a recognition that income is a distribution, not a guarantee. It is the discipline of aligning rigidity with what can be depended upon across normal fluctuations. It transforms projected income from structural support into optional enhancement.

When this distinction is embedded into financial architecture, income variability ceases to be destabilizing within ordinary bands. Peaks create opportunity without inflating baseline commitments. Troughs reduce surplus without threatening foundational stability.

The result is structural coherence across cycles.

Reliable income defines the boundary of safe commitment. Projected income defines the range of potential enhancement. Confusing the two narrows tolerance invisibly. Distinguishing them preserves autonomy across time.

Financial control begins not with earning more, but with knowing which portion of income can be trusted to carry weight.

There is an additional dimension to reliability that becomes visible only when income is evaluated across stress intervals rather than stable ones.

Most income histories are examined during expansionary periods. Performance is assessed relative to favorable conditions. Yet the true test of reliability occurs during constraint. How does income behave when demand softens, when markets tighten, when institutional priorities shift, or when personal performance encounters ordinary variability?

Income that remains stable across mild stress intervals possesses a narrower volatility band than income that contracts sharply under the same conditions. The reliable floor must be informed by these stress intervals, not solely by neutral or favorable periods.

This does not require forecasting severe recession or catastrophic events. It requires acknowledging that ordinary stress recurs. Industries cool. Employers restructure. Incentives are reduced. Clients delay discretionary projects. These are cyclical features of economic life.

If income contracts meaningfully during such intervals, that contraction must be incorporated into the reliable floor calculation. Ignoring it creates an artificial baseline that will not hold when conditions normalize.

The professional who distinguishes reliability from projection evaluates income history longitudinally rather than selectively. Peaks are observed, but troughs are weighted more heavily in structural calibration. The lower bound is not dismissed as anomaly unless there is credible evidence that underlying income structure has changed permanently.

This disciplined weighting produces a conservative reliable floor relative to recent highs. It may feel restrictive in prosperous periods because it constrains commitment expansion. Yet it produces stability across full cycles rather than within isolated segments.

Income volatility bands can also widen due to internal choices, not only external conditions. Shifting toward performance-heavy compensation structures, launching entrepreneurial ventures, or concentrating revenue among fewer clients can increase peak income while widening the band.

If the volatility band widens, the reliable floor may remain unchanged even as average income rises. Commitments anchored to rising averages without regard to widening bands increase exposure.

Exposure here is not speculative. It is structural. The system becomes more sensitive to variance because a greater portion of commitments depends on uncertain inflow.

Reliability as a design principle demands recalibration when volatility bands widen. If income becomes more variable, the reliable floor may need to be lowered rather than raised, even if recent realized income has increased. This is counterintuitive but structurally necessary.

For example, a professional moving from a stable salaried role into an entrepreneurial structure may double average annual income. Yet if the new structure introduces significant variance across months or years, the reliable floor may initially approximate prior salary rather than new peaks. Anchoring commitments to the doubled average would embed projection into rigidity.

Over time, if recurring revenue stabilizes and variance narrows, the reliable floor can legitimately rise. Until then, discipline requires separation between realized peaks and dependable baseline.

The failure to distinguish these phases often leads to instability in transitional careers. Early entrepreneurial success produces elevated income. Commitments expand rapidly. When revenue fluctuates in subsequent periods—as is common during growth—the system experiences compression. What appeared to be success reveals structural fragility.

A reliability-based approach would treat early peaks as provisional until volatility bands narrow demonstrably. Commitment expansion would lag revenue expansion. This lag preserves tolerance during formative stages.

Reliability also interacts with taxation and withholding patterns. Variable income often produces variable tax obligations. If projected income is assumed to persist, tax reserves may be calibrated too tightly. When realized income declines, prior tax assumptions may create additional strain. The volatility band extends beyond gross income into net availability.

Thus the reliable floor must be assessed after considering structural deductions that fluctuate alongside income. Net reliable income, not gross projection, supports rigid commitments.

Over extended time horizons, reliability-based design reduces amplitude of lifestyle oscillation. Lifestyle oscillation occurs when spending expands during high-income periods and contracts during lower-income periods. Oscillation generates instability not only financially but psychologically. Repeated expansion and contraction erode perceived control.

When rigid commitments remain anchored to reliable floors, lifestyle oscillation is dampened. Surplus may fluctuate, but baseline commitments remain steady. Adjustments occur in optional domains rather than in core structure.

This dampening effect compounds stability. It reduces the need for abrupt contraction during downturns and prevents rapid escalation during upswings. The system evolves gradually rather than episodically.

Gradual evolution produces coherence.

Coherence is the alignment between dependable inflow and fixed outflow across time. It reflects structural proportionality rather than peak performance. When coherence is maintained, income variability does not translate into structural disruption.

Reliability, then, is not caution against ambition. It is insulation against volatility. It allows professionals to pursue variable upside without mortgaging stability to its continuation.

Income projections will always exist. Expectations are unavoidable in career planning and business development. The architectural question is not whether to project, but whether to embed projections into rigidity.

When projection remains distinct from reliability, upside remains opportunity. When projection becomes baseline, upside becomes obligation.

Financial control depends on keeping those categories separate.

Reliable income defines what the system can safely carry. Projected income defines what the system may temporarily enjoy. The boundary between them is not emotional. It is statistical and structural.

Where that boundary is drawn determines whether prosperity widens stability or conceals fragility.

There is a practical implication that emerges when reliability is treated as structural rather than emotional: commitment growth must follow demonstrated stability, not precede it.

Demonstrated stability is evidenced by sustained narrowing of volatility bands across varied conditions. If income remains elevated not only during expansion but also during moderate contraction, if variability decreases because compensation structure has shifted toward fixed components or recurring contracts, then the reliable floor rises legitimately. Commitment recalibration can follow.

If income rises but volatility remains wide, commitment recalibration must wait.

This lag between income growth and commitment growth is often misinterpreted as restraint or underutilization of earning capacity. Structurally, it is stabilization. It allows income distribution to reveal its true band before rigidity expands to meet it.

Without this lag, projection drift accelerates. Recent prosperity is encoded into baseline expectation. Each new commitment embeds a fraction of upside into structural necessity. Over time, baseline commitments migrate toward peak income. When income mean-reverts toward the lower bound, the gap is exposed.

This pattern is not rare. It is cyclical across industries and career stages. High-earning professionals frequently encounter periods where realized income falls 10 to 30 percent below recent peaks. If commitments were expanded during peak cycles, the compression is immediate and structural.

If commitments were anchored to reliable floors, the same contraction reduces surplus rather than threatening obligations.

The asymmetry becomes decisive over long time horizons. Systems that embed upside into rigidity must repeatedly adjust during downturns. Each adjustment carries transaction cost—financial, strategic, and psychological. Systems that preserve upside as optional capacity accumulate stability during expansion and maintain it during contraction.

The cumulative effect of these divergent paths is not subtle. Over decades, reliability-based systems retain control through cycles. Projection-based systems experience periodic strain even if average income is high.

Reliability also imposes clarity in professional decision-making. When evaluating a new opportunity with higher but more variable compensation, the question becomes whether the reliable floor will rise, fall, or remain constant. If variability increases without increasing dependable baseline, commitments should not expand merely because average income may rise.

This prevents a common structural error: expanding fixed obligations based on aspirational averages tied to unproven compensation structures.

Conversely, if a new role increases fixed salary significantly while reducing variability, the reliable floor may rise even if peak income declines.

In such cases, stability increases despite lower potential upside. The structural effect is positive because volatility band narrows.

Income evaluation must therefore incorporate both magnitude and dispersion. Magnitude without dispersion analysis obscures risk. Dispersion without magnitude analysis ignores capacity. Reliability integrates both by focusing on dependable lower bounds.

When reliability becomes embedded as a design principle, financial architecture stabilizes across cycles. Commitments are justified against what can be depended upon, not what has recently been achieved. Upside enhances capacity rather than underwriting obligation. Downside compresses surplus rather than threatening coherence.

The distinction between reliable income and projected income is therefore foundational. It defines what the system can safely carry. It separates structural support from contingent enhancement.

Where that separation is ignored, instability is introduced quietly during prosperity and revealed abruptly during variance.

Where that separation is respected, stability is accumulated gradually and preserved across fluctuation.

Financial control rests on that boundary.

Obligation Rigidity and Margin Calibration

Income defines capacity. Obligations define constraint. Stability is determined by how those two are proportioned and structured across time.

Obligations are not uniform. They vary in rigidity. Rigidity is the degree to which a commitment resists adjustment in timing, magnitude, or duration without external consequence. Financial architecture must distinguish among fixed, semi-fixed, and flexible commitments because each exerts different structural pressure on the system.

Fixed commitments are contractually bound in both amount and schedule. Housing payments under long-term lease or mortgage, installment agreements, insurance premiums with defined payment dates—these obligations demand compliance. Their timing is externally imposed. Their magnitude is predetermined. Deviation triggers penalty or loss of access.

Semi-fixed commitments occupy an intermediate position. They recur predictably but allow limited adjustment. Utilities may fluctuate within a range. Service subscriptions may be cancellable but with notice periods. Tuition installments may offer short deferrals but not elimination. These obligations are partially elastic but still exert structural weight.

Flexible commitments are discretionary. They can be adjusted rapidly without contractual consequence. Dining, travel, elective purchases, and certain categories of lifestyle spending fall into this domain. Their magnitude and timing can be altered immediately without systemic breach.

The distinction matters because only fixed and semi-fixed commitments constitute structural load in a strict sense. Flexible spending influences cash flow but does not create external enforcement.

Stability depends on the proportion of reliable income absorbed by rigid commitments—fixed and semi-fixed combined. As rigidity increases, the system's tolerance to income variance narrows. As flexibility increases, tolerance widens.

Contract duration multiplies rigidity.

A one-year lease and a thirty-year mortgage may represent similar monthly obligations, but their structural implications differ significantly. Duration extends exposure. The longer the commitment horizon, the greater the probability that income conditions will vary during its life. A long-duration obligation embeds expectation about future income stability across extended cycles.

Duration does not alter monthly load; it alters persistence. Short-term rigidity can be recalibrated periodically. Long-term rigidity locks in assumptions across economic environments.

For example, a professional may commit to a five-year commercial lease based on current revenue strength. If revenue volatility widens in year three, the lease remains binding. The duration of the commitment amplifies miscalibration because adjustment cannot occur without cost.

Thus rigidity is not only magnitude but temporal length.

Obligation density adds another dimension. Density refers to the concentration of rigid commitments relative to reliable income. When multiple fixed commitments consume a high proportion of dependable inflow, density increases. High density reduces structural slack.

Density must also be considered in time clustering. If several rigid commitments share similar due periods, even a structurally adequate aggregate margin may experience periodic compression. Clustering concentrates structural pressure at specific intervals.

While total rigidity load determines baseline tolerance, clustering determines episodic strain. A system with moderate overall rigidity but heavy temporal clustering may experience recurring stress despite acceptable aggregate proportions.

Margin is the structural distance between the reliable income floor and total rigid load. It is not surplus in a casual sense. It is the protective gap that absorbs income variance without threatening commitments.

If reliable monthly income is $10,000 and fixed plus semi-fixed obligations total $8,500, the margin is $1,500. That distance defines how much contraction can occur before commitments are at risk. If rigid load rises to $9,700, the margin narrows to $300. Tolerance declines sharply even though income magnitude remains unchanged.

Margin is therefore a design variable. It is not discovered after obligations are chosen; it is created through calibration.

Gradual rigidity accumulation often occurs during prosperity. Income rises. New commitments appear manageable. A higher housing cost is justified by increased compensation. Additional service contracts are layered in. Financing replaces upfront purchases. Each commitment appears sustainable in isolation.

Collectively, they compress margin.

Because prosperity masks volatility, accumulation feels efficient. Reliable floor and projected income converge temporarily, making rigid load appear well within capacity. Yet if rigid commitments expand toward projected peaks rather than reliable floors, margin narrows invisibly.

When variance returns, the reduced margin becomes apparent. What had felt comfortable now feels constrained.

This dynamic illustrates the efficiency versus elasticity trade-off.

Efficiency seeks to maximize utilization of income. It minimizes unused capacity. In purely arithmetic terms, efficiency appears optimal: resources are fully deployed, lifestyle reflects earning power, fixed costs align closely with realized income.

Elasticity seeks to preserve structural slack. It tolerates unused capacity in exchange for variance absorption. In strictly numerical terms, elasticity may appear suboptimal because margin represents income not converted into immediate lifestyle expansion.

However, elasticity provides resilience.

A highly efficient system operates near full utilization of reliable income. It is optimized for stable conditions. A highly elastic system operates below full utilization. It sacrifices some current consumption to preserve structural tolerance.

The appropriate balance depends on income volatility and duration of commitments. In highly stable compensation structures with narrow volatility bands and short commitment horizons, efficiency may not significantly endanger stability. In variable compensation structures with long-duration commitments, elasticity becomes essential.

Proportional rigidity is the principle that rigid load should scale cautiously relative to reliable income floor. As reliable income rises, rigid commitments may rise—but not at the same rate unless volatility has demonstrably narrowed.

If reliable income increases by 20 percent but volatility band remains unchanged, increasing rigid load by 20 percent preserves density and margin proportionally. Increasing rigid load by 30 percent reduces margin despite higher income.

Scaling must therefore be measured relative to dependable capacity, not peak earnings.

Proportional rigidity preserves structural balance as magnitude changes. It prevents the common pattern in which income growth leads to accelerated rigidity growth, eroding tolerance over time.

Calibration is not a one-time decision. It is continuous.

Income evolves. Obligations evolve. Market conditions evolve. Each new commitment alters rigidity density and margin. Each income shift alters reliable floor and structural distance.

A system that was calibrated conservatively at one stage may become tightly coupled later if commitments accumulate gradually without re-evaluating margin. Similarly, a system that begins tightly configured may widen tolerance if income structure stabilizes and rigidity remains controlled.

Calibration requires periodic structural review: assessing reliable income floor, measuring total rigid load including semi-fixed commitments, evaluating duration exposure, and determining margin distance.

This review is not emotional. It is mechanical.

When rigid commitments remain anchored below reliable floors with adequate margin distance, the system maintains tolerance. When rigid commitments drift upward toward projected income, margin narrows and exposure increases.

Obligation rigidity is neither inherently negative nor inherently positive. It provides stability in exchange for flexibility. Long-term housing commitments, for example, may offer cost predictability. Insurance contracts provide defined protection. Rigidity can reduce variability in certain domains.

The structural issue is proportion and calibration.

When rigidity is proportionate to dependable income and balanced with sufficient margin, it enhances stability. When rigidity exceeds dependable income or clusters excessively, it transforms variability into risk.

Financial control depends on managing this proportion deliberately rather than allowing it to drift during prosperity.

Rigid commitments determine how much of reliable income is already spoken for before discretionary decisions are made. Margin determines how much variation can occur without structural disruption. Duration determines how long assumptions are locked in. Density determines how concentrated obligations are relative to dependable capacity.

Together, these variables define the structural behavior of the system under variance.

When margin is wide, rigidity proportionate, and duration aligned with volatility, the system remains coherent even when income fluctuates. When margin is narrow, rigidity dense, and duration extended beyond reliability, the system becomes sensitive.

Calibration is the mechanism by which these elements are balanced across time.

Rigidity rarely increases through a single dramatic decision. It accumulates incrementally.

A housing upgrade adds one layer. A financed vehicle adds another. A long-term service agreement appears modest relative to total income. Educational commitments, subscription layers, maintenance contracts, installment plans—each introduces a new fixed or semi-fixed obligation. None independently destabilizes the system. Collectively, they compress margin.

This gradual accumulation is often invisible because income growth accompanies it. As reliable income rises, new commitments feel justified. The structural error occurs when rigidity grows slightly faster than dependable capacity or when duration lengthens without corresponding reduction in volatility.

Rigidity accumulation under prosperity is particularly subtle because variance appears low during favorable cycles. When income is consistently strong, the distinction between reliable floor and projected expectation becomes psychologically blurred. Commitments expand toward recent realized income rather than toward statistically dependable baseline.

The system appears stable because realized income supports rigid load. Structural vulnerability remains latent until income reverts toward the lower bound of its volatility band.

At that point, margin recalibration is required under pressure.

When rigid commitments approach reliable income floor too closely, flexibility absorbs the initial contraction. Discretionary spending is reduced. Savings rates decline. Optional allocations are deferred. If contraction persists, semi-fixed commitments are scrutinized. Eventually, structural commitments themselves may require adjustment—through refinancing, downsizing, or renegotiation.

Each of these adjustments carries friction.

Friction is not limited to financial cost. It includes time, negotiation complexity, reputational considerations, and strategic constraint. Long-duration obligations resist adjustment precisely when adjustment is most needed.

The longer the duration and the higher the rigidity density, the slower the system adapts.

This interaction between duration and density amplifies risk. A high-density system composed primarily of short-duration commitments can recalibrate periodically. A high-density system composed of long-duration commitments becomes locked.

Elasticity depends on having either lower density or shorter duration. When both density and duration are high, structural flexibility declines sharply.

The efficiency versus elasticity trade-off becomes visible here. Efficiency optimizes for present utilization of income. It reduces idle capacity. Elasticity preserves unused capacity to absorb variance.

In prosperous conditions, efficiency appears rational. Underutilized margin feels inefficient. There is pressure to convert available capacity into tangible upgrades. Yet the act of converting margin into rigidity reduces elasticity.

Elasticity is not waste. It is deferred consumption in exchange for variance tolerance.

The professional must decide how much elasticity is appropriate relative to volatility. In low-volatility, high-reliability environments with short commitment horizons, higher efficiency may be sustainable. In variable environments or when commitments span long durations, elasticity becomes protective.

The trade-off is dynamic. It shifts as income structure changes.

If a professional's reliable income floor rises and volatility narrows, proportional rigidity can increase without reducing margin. If volatility widens, rigidity may need to contract proportionally to maintain margin distance.

Proportional rigidity functions as a scaling principle. As dependable income grows, rigid commitments may grow—but always in measured proportion to reliable floor, not projected peak. If reliable floor grows by 10 percent and volatility remains constant, rigid commitments might grow by a smaller percentage to widen margin gradually.

Widening margin across income growth cycles produces cumulative stability. It prevents rigidity density from creeping upward unnoticed.

When rigidity grows faster than reliable floor, margin narrows even as income rises. This produces a paradoxical experience: higher income with unchanged or increased stress.

This paradox is common among high-earning professionals. Income has grown substantially over a decade. Yet perceived financial pressure has not decreased. The explanation often lies in proportional rigidity. Commitments expanded to match or exceed reliable income growth, eliminating margin gains.

Calibration must therefore be continuous, not episodic.

Each new commitment alters density. Each income shift alters reliable floor. Each contract duration extends exposure across time. Calibration involves assessing whether rigid load remains comfortably below dependable income and whether duration aligns with volatility expectations.

This assessment is structural, not moral. It does not require minimizing commitments. It requires ensuring that commitments are supported by dependable capacity.

Semi-fixed commitments deserve particular scrutiny because they often escape attention. Subscriptions, maintenance plans, recurring services, installment arrangements—each may be individually small. Collectively, they increase density and reduce margin. Because they are cancellable, they are perceived as flexible. Yet cancellation often requires notice, renegotiation, or disruption. Semi-fixed obligations thus exert more structural weight than flexible spending.

High semi-fixed density can mimic fixed rigidity under stress. If multiple semi-fixed commitments must be unwound simultaneously, friction accumulates. The system behaves as if rigidity were higher than assumed.

Effective calibration accounts for semi-fixed load alongside fixed commitments when measuring margin distance.

Margin, in structural terms, is not merely the difference between income and expenses in a typical month. It is the distance between reliable floor and total rigid load across time. A wide margin absorbs income contraction. A narrow margin requires immediate adaptation.

Margin also determines how aggressively a professional can pursue variable opportunities. When margin is wide, income volatility can be tolerated without threatening obligations. When margin is narrow, stable income becomes mandatory, constraining strategic choice.

Thus obligation rigidity and margin calibration influence career posture as well as financial stress.

Over long horizons, systems that preserve margin accumulate optionality. Systems that compress margin in pursuit of efficiency become dependent on stable or growing income to remain coherent.

The discipline of calibration ensures that rigidity remains proportional to dependable capacity rather than to recent prosperity.

This discipline is not static. It must adjust when reliable floor shifts, when volatility changes, and when long-duration commitments are introduced. Without continuous recalibration, incremental rigidity accumulation can quietly erode tolerance even in the absence of obvious financial strain.

Structural stability is maintained not by avoiding obligations, but by aligning their magnitude and duration with dependable income and preserving sufficient margin distance to absorb variance.

Rigidity defines constraint. Margin defines tolerance. Calibration aligns the two.

Rigidity is often defended on the grounds of predictability. A fixed housing payment, a long-term contract, or a multi-year financing arrangement can reduce certain forms of uncertainty. The payment amount is known. The schedule is known. In isolation, predictability appears stabilizing.

The structural question is whether the predictability of the obligation is matched by the predictability of the income supporting it.

When rigid commitments are supported by highly reliable income with narrow volatility bands, predictability compounds predictability. The system becomes steady. When rigid commitments are supported by income with wider variance, predictability in outflow collides with variability in inflow. The mismatch creates structural tension.

Thus rigidity is not inherently destabilizing. It becomes destabilizing when it is disproportionate to dependable inflow.

Obligation density intensifies this dynamic. If a single rigid commitment consumes a modest portion of reliable income, the system can absorb temporary variance through flexibility elsewhere. If multiple rigid commitments collectively consume the majority of dependable income, variance has nowhere to be absorbed except through structural contraction.

Clustering magnifies density. Even if rigid commitments represent an acceptable proportion of reliable income in aggregate, temporal concentration can create effective overexposure during specific intervals. If a large percentage of rigid payments are due within a narrow timeframe, short-term liquidity strain can emerge despite adequate long-term margin.

Density across time and density in aggregate must both be considered.

Margin functions as a buffer not only against magnitude variance but also against duration risk. Long-duration commitments embed assumptions about future reliable income. The longer the duration, the more economic cycles the commitment will span. Margin provides room for those cycles to unfold without immediate breach.

A system with minimal margin may operate smoothly in stable conditions but lacks tolerance for ordinary cyclical contraction. A system with ample margin can endure moderate downturns without restructuring commitments.

The concept of proportional rigidity becomes decisive as professionals advance in career and income level. Early in a career, commitments are often smaller in magnitude but can still represent high proportions of reliable income. Later, as income grows, commitments expand. The danger lies not in expansion itself but in the rate of expansion relative to dependable capacity.

If rigid commitments grow faster than reliable income floor, proportional rigidity increases. Even if absolute margin appears stable in nominal terms, the system becomes more sensitive to percentage contractions in income.

For example, if reliable income floor rises from $80,000 to $120,000 and rigid commitments rise from $60,000 to $105,000, nominal margin has increased from $20,000 to $15,000 negative? Wait example: 80-60=20; 120-105=15. Margin narrowed despite income growth. Percentage-wise, rigidity moved from 75 percent to 87.5 percent of reliable floor. Sensitivity to income contraction increased.

The professional may perceive greater prosperity because income is higher. Structurally, tolerance has declined.

This is the subtlety of proportional rigidity. It measures commitment growth relative to dependable capacity, not relative to prior lifestyle.

Gradual rigidity accumulation often disguises itself as normalization. Each new fixed cost becomes part of baseline. What was once discretionary becomes essential. Services that began as optional integrate into routine. Over time, the system's baseline rises.

If baseline rises to the edge of reliable floor, elasticity disappears. The system becomes fully utilized. Any income fluctuation forces contraction not from luxury but from baseline commitments.

Efficiency at full utilization may feel optimal during expansion. It eliminates perceived waste. Yet full utilization eliminates slack. Slack is the structural distance that allows recalibration without disruption.

Elastic systems preserve slack deliberately. They accept some underutilized capacity in exchange for adaptability.

The trade-off between efficiency and elasticity is therefore strategic. It depends on the volatility of income, the duration of commitments, and the professional's tolerance for constraint.

A professional in a highly stable field with predictable salary progression may rationally operate with higher rigidity density than one in a volatile entrepreneurial domain. However, even in stable domains, macroeconomic shifts, industry disruption, or organizational restructuring can widen volatility unexpectedly. Excessive efficiency leaves little room for such shifts.

Calibration must incorporate not only observed volatility but also plausible volatility.

Plausibility is not worst-case speculation. It is recognition that historical volatility provides a guide but not a guarantee. When commitments extend across decades, income conditions are unlikely to remain static. Margin protects against this inevitability.

Calibration is therefore a continuous design decision. It must respond to shifts in income structure, life stage, and commitment profile.

When reliable income floor increases demonstrably and volatility narrows, margin can widen even as commitments expand. When volatility increases, margin should widen further by restraining rigidity growth. When duration of commitments lengthens, margin should widen to compensate for extended exposure.

Failure to recalibrate leads to structural drift. Drift occurs when commitments accumulate faster than dependable capacity, not through a single decision but through incremental additions that seem justified at the time.

Drift reduces tolerance invisibly. Because each addition is small relative to total income, the cumulative effect is overlooked. Only when income variance reasserts itself does the reduced margin become apparent.

The professional then confronts rigidity that cannot be easily unwound.

Structural control requires resisting drift through periodic measurement of rigid load against reliable floor and through deliberate preservation of margin distance.

Obligation rigidity is not an enemy of stability. It provides structure and predictability. But it must be proportionate, duration-aware, and margin-supported.

Margin is the measurable expression of tolerance. It defines how much contraction can occur before commitments are stressed. The wider the margin, the broader the range of survivable conditions.

Calibration aligns rigidity with reliable income floor and preserves sufficient margin to absorb variance across time.

When rigidity remains proportionate and margin remains deliberate, prosperity strengthens the system rather than tightening it. When rigidity drifts upward unchecked, prosperity narrows tolerance and sets the stage for compression under variance.

Structural durability depends on continuous alignment between dependable capacity and committed load.

That alignment is not accidental. It is designed.

Over extended time horizons, obligation rigidity shapes the character of a financial life more than income volatility alone. Income may fluctuate within bands. Rigidity determines how consequential those fluctuations become.

When rigid load is calibrated conservatively relative to dependable capacity, income variability is experienced as change in surplus. When rigid load approaches dependable capacity, income variability is experienced as threat. The psychological difference is significant, but its origin is structural.

Rigid commitments convert income into obligation before discretion is applied. The larger the conversion, the smaller the discretionary domain. When discretion narrows excessively, even minor variance reduces autonomy.

Autonomy, in structural terms, is the ability to adjust without violating commitments.

High rigidity reduces autonomy because adjustment options are limited. Flexible categories can absorb only so much contraction before quality of life is impaired. If rigid load is high enough, contraction must eventually target core commitments, which often require renegotiation or external approval.

Low to moderate rigidity preserves autonomy. Flexible categories can absorb variance without destabilizing the system. Margin remains intact. Decision-making remains internal.

This autonomy compounds over time. Professionals with preserved autonomy can choose when to expand commitments and when to maintain slack. They are not forced to align career decisions with immediate income requirements because rigid load does not dominate dependable capacity.

Rigidity also interacts with life stage transitions. Marriage, family expansion, relocation, career shifts, and entrepreneurial experimentation all introduce variability. A system with high rigidity density enters such transitions with limited flexibility. A system with calibrated rigidity and preserved margin enters with tolerance.

Transitions rarely align with perfect income stability. They often coincide with temporary income dips, relocation costs, or career uncertainty. If rigid load has been scaled aggressively during prior prosperity, the transition window becomes narrow. If margin has been preserved, the transition can unfold without structural strain.

Proportional rigidity must therefore account not only for current income volatility but also for anticipated life variability.

Anticipation does not require forecasting specific events. It requires acknowledging that change is inevitable over long durations. Long-term commitments will span multiple economic and personal cycles. Margin is the design mechanism that absorbs those cycles.

Calibration as a continuous decision means that rigidity is never allowed to drift unchecked. Each commitment is evaluated against dependable income, existing density, and duration exposure. Each income change prompts reassessment of margin distance.

This ongoing discipline prevents the system from becoming tightly configured without awareness. It ensures that prosperity widens structural tolerance rather than erodes it.

When reliable income floor rises, margin can widen first before rigidity expands. When rigidity expands, it does so proportionately, leaving adequate distance from dependable capacity. When volatility increases, rigidity growth pauses or contracts to maintain tolerance.

This dynamic equilibrium produces durable stability.

Durable stability is not the absence of obligation. It is the presence of proportion. It is the deliberate spacing between what is committed and what is dependable. It is the refusal to equate present prosperity with permanent capacity.

Obligation rigidity, margin distance, duration exposure, and density interact continuously. If managed deliberately, they create a system that remains coherent across variation. If left to drift during favorable conditions, they narrow tolerance invisibly.

Financial control is sustained not by eliminating rigidity but by calibrating it. Rigidity provides structure. Margin provides protection. Proportion provides balance.

Where rigid load is aligned with reliable income floor and supported by adequate margin across time, income variance alters comfort but not stability.

Where rigid load encroaches upon dependable capacity, income variance alters stability itself.

The architecture of durability rests on that distinction.

Margin Compression and Structural Drift

Margin compression is the narrowing of structural distance between the reliable income floor and total rigid load across time. It is not an event. It is a progression. It does not announce itself through missed payments or visible financial stress. It advances quietly while income rises, obligations are met, and outward stability appears intact.

Margin is the measurable space between dependable capacity and committed load. When that space contracts, tolerance contracts. The system's ability to absorb variance without structural reconfiguration declines. This can occur without insolvency. It can occur without late payments. It can occur during periods of income growth.

Solvency is the ability to meet obligations as they come due. Tolerance is the ability to continue meeting those obligations under deviation from expected conditions. A system can remain solvent while becoming progressively less tolerant. Margin compression is the process by which that decline in tolerance unfolds.

The distinction is critical because solvency is observable in the present. Tolerance is revealed only under variance. A solvent system that has experienced compression will appear stable under steady input and fragile under moderate disruption.

Two primary drivers produce compression.

The first is rigidity rising faster than the reliable income floor. Income may increase in nominal terms, but if fixed and semi-fixed commitments expand more rapidly than dependable capacity, structural distance narrows. This may occur when projected income is treated as stable and commitments are calibrated to recent peaks rather than to reliable floor.

The second driver is reliable floor stagnating while rigidity accumulates. Income volatility may widen or plateau. The dependable baseline may not increase materially. Yet commitments continue to layer incrementally. Even without lifestyle expansion, semi-fixed additions and duration extensions can compress margin relative to dependable capacity.

Both drivers can operate simultaneously. Income may grow modestly while rigidity grows aggressively. Or income may plateau while rigidity grows gradually. In both cases, margin declines proportionally.

Structural drift is the mechanism through which compression becomes normalized.

Drift does not require conscious overextension. It emerges from incremental commitment layering without proportional recalibration. Each decision appears reasonable within its immediate context. A service is added because it improves efficiency. A financing arrangement is extended because it lowers monthly burden. A contract is renewed automatically because it remains affordable.

No single decision materially alters the structure. The cumulative effect does.

Drift converts slack into obligation gradually. It narrows structural distance without triggering alarm because the narrowing is incremental. Income growth can obscure drift by maintaining positive cash flow even as margin contracts.

Semi-fixed creep functions as a primary drift engine.

Recurring subscriptions, structured service plans, installment arrangements, maintenance programs, bundled memberships, and auto-renewed contracts accumulate over time. Each is individually modest relative to total income. Collectively, they increase rigidity density.

Under stable conditions, semi-fixed commitments feel flexible. They are technically cancellable. Under stress, however, unwinding multiple semi-fixed obligations requires time, administrative effort, and lifestyle adjustment. Notice periods, cancellation penalties, and dependency on services transform semi-fixed commitments into practical rigidity.

Under variance, semi-fixed creep behaves as fixed load.

Because semi-fixed obligations are often categorized psychologically as discretionary, their structural weight is underestimated. In aggregate, they compress margin by occupying dependable capacity that might otherwise remain elastic.

Duration layering is a second drift engine.

Long-term commitments stack across time. A mortgage is layered with an auto loan. An education financing agreement is layered with a renovation loan. A business lease overlaps with equipment financing. Each layer extends assumptions about future dependable income.

Duration does not increase monthly load necessarily; it extends exposure. The longer the contract stack, the more economic cycles the system must traverse while maintaining sufficient reliable income to support commitments.

Duration layering multiplies compression because it reduces the frequency at which recalibration can occur. Short-duration commitments allow periodic restructuring. Long-duration commitments lock in structural assumptions for years or decades.

When duration increases without widening margin proportionally, future volatility risk intensifies.

Density and clustering function as compression multipliers.

Density refers to the percentage of dependable capacity already spoken for by rigid and semi-fixed commitments. As density rises, discretionary domain shrinks. When a high proportion of reliable floor is allocated to non-adjustable obligations, tolerance for income variance declines.

Clustering refers to the concentration of obligations within specific time windows. Even if aggregate rigidity density is manageable, temporal concentration can create localized compression. When large portions of dependable capacity are due within narrow periods, minor inflow variance can produce disproportionate strain.

Density and clustering interact. High density with dispersed timing is less fragile than high density with concentrated timing. However, both reduce margin relative to reliable floor.

Hidden compression differs from acute shock.

Acute shock is visible. Income drops sharply or expenses surge unexpectedly, and obligations cannot be met without immediate adjustment. Hidden compression is invisible until variance appears. It is the narrowing of tolerance during stable conditions.

Stable-but-brittle architecture results when hidden compression advances without visible instability. The system performs well under expected input. It lacks slack to absorb deviation.

Tolerance narrows before instability appears.

Behavioral and system symptoms emerge as compression progresses.

Response windows shorten. In wide-margin systems, moderate variance can be absorbed across multiple cycles without structural change. In compressed systems, even small deviations require prompt action because margin is insufficient to allow delay.

Sequencing sensitivity increases. With less structural distance, timing mismatches between inflow and outflow exert greater pressure. Minor delays require immediate compensation.

Liquidity substitution becomes more frequent. Instead of absorbing variance structurally, the system shifts funds tactically. Internal transfers, temporary buffer drawdowns, or short-term liquidity sources bridge small gaps. The architecture remains intact, but reliance on liquidity management increases.

Slower recovery velocity becomes evident. After a minor disturbance, the system takes longer to return to baseline surplus levels. Margin that once rebuilt quickly now rebuilds slowly because it is narrower.

Cognitive load rises. Monitoring intensifies. Financial management consumes greater attention even though income magnitude may be high. The system demands precision to remain stable.

These symptoms are structural, not emotional.

Early warning indicators appear before overt stress.

If rigid and semi-fixed load as a percentage of reliable floor increases year over year, compression is occurring.

If discretionary domain shrinks consistently to preserve baseline commitments, elasticity is declining.

If contract stack duration lengthens through overlapping long-term obligations without corresponding increase in dependable capacity, exposure is increasing.

If recovery from small disturbances takes multiple cycles when it previously required one, margin has narrowed.

If income growth is consistently translated into commitment growth without observable widening of structural distance, drift is underway.

These indicators do not require crisis to be visible. They require measurement.

Prevention rests on a simple principle: margin must widen before rigidity expands.

When reliable floor increases, structural distance should increase first. Growth in dependable capacity should expand tolerance before being converted into new long-term commitments. Only after margin has widened materially should selective rigidity expansion occur, and even then proportionally.

Growth should widen tolerance before scaling commitments.

Without this discipline, prosperity becomes the engine of compression. Slack feels inefficient. Income increases invite utilization. Commitments expand reflexively. Margin contracts quietly.

Maintenance discipline interrupts drift.

Periodic structural review must reassess reliable floor relative to current volatility, measure total rigid and semi-fixed load, evaluate duration stack distribution, and calculate margin distance explicitly.

Scenario modeling of moderate variance should test whether commitments remain secure across multiple cycles without tactical intervention. If moderate contraction would require immediate structural adjustment, margin is insufficient.

Maintenance is not crisis management. It is preservation of structural distance.

Margin compression alters not only financial mechanics but temporal perception. As tolerance narrows, the system becomes increasingly present-oriented. Decisions are evaluated against immediate cash impact rather than multi-cycle coherence. The future is still planned for, but planning is constrained by near-term rigidity. This shift is not cognitive bias. It is structural necessity.

Durable stability requires measurable space between dependable capacity and committed load. When that space is preserved and widened deliberately, variance becomes manageable. When that space narrows incrementally, stability becomes conditional.

Margin is the structural expression of tolerance. Compression reduces it. Drift erodes it. Maintenance preserves it.

Compression also alters how variance propagates through the system.

In wide-margin configurations, variance tends to localize. A moderate income shortfall reduces surplus accumulation. A temporary expense increase delays optional allocation. The disturbance is absorbed within a contained domain. Core commitments remain insulated because structural distance exists.

In compressed configurations, variance does not localize. It propagates.

When rigid load occupies a high percentage of reliable floor, any income deviation immediately interacts with committed obligations. There is insufficient discretionary domain to contain the disturbance. What would have been a surplus reduction becomes a structural tension. The disturbance moves from optional categories toward baseline commitments more quickly.

Propagation speed increases as margin narrows.

This acceleration matters because it reduces the time available for corrective action. In preserved systems, variance can be observed, evaluated, and responded to gradually. In compressed systems, response must be immediate. The window between disturbance and structural pressure shortens.

Shortened windows increase reliance on tactical solutions. Liquidity is reallocated. Payments are sequenced more precisely. Timing becomes central. The system can remain solvent through careful management, but it is no longer tolerant.

Tolerance is the capacity to absorb without intervention. Solvency under constant intervention is not equivalent.

As compression deepens, even positive deviations can produce structural stress. A one-time large expense tied to opportunity—professional development, relocation, investment—may strain liquidity because margin is insufficient to absorb it. The system becomes cautious not only in downturns but also in growth phases.

This inversion is significant. In preserved systems, growth events are easier to integrate because slack exists. In compressed systems, growth events compete with existing rigidity for limited structural space.

Duration layering intensifies propagation.

When long-term commitments stack across multiple domains—housing, transportation, education, business infrastructure—the number of fixed constraints increases. Each constraint reduces degrees of freedom. When variance appears, adjustment options are limited because many obligations are locked in for extended periods.

If margin is wide, duration layering may be sustainable because structural distance buffers exposure. If margin is narrow, duration layering locks the system into rigid pathways.

Density concentration further accelerates propagation. When a large share of reliable floor is already allocated to fixed and semi-fixed commitments, variance cannot be absorbed through flexible categories alone. Flexible categories may represent too small a percentage of total outflow to offset even modest income contraction.

At that point, either commitments must be renegotiated or liquidity substitution must occur. Both introduce friction.

Friction slows recovery velocity. Recovery velocity is the number of cycles required for the system to return to its prior structural position after disturbance. In preserved systems, recovery velocity is high—few cycles are needed. In compressed systems, recovery velocity declines. Disturbances leave residual effects that persist.

Residual effects accumulate when disturbances occur before full recovery. Because variance is continuous rather than singular, compressed systems often operate in partial recovery state. Margin never fully rebuilds. Slack remains thin.

This persistent near-limit operation increases cognitive load further. Monitoring becomes habitual. Precision is demanded. Attention is diverted from structural design toward operational balancing.

Operational balancing is energy-intensive and does not widen margin.

Another secondary effect emerges in how professionals evaluate new commitments.

In preserved systems, new commitments are evaluated against structural distance. The question is whether margin remains adequate after inclusion. In compressed systems, new commitments are evaluated primarily against monthly affordability under current income. Because structural distance is already narrow, focus shifts to immediate cash impact rather than to long-term tolerance.

This shift is subtle but consequential. It reinforces compression by ignoring proportional rigidity and duration exposure.

Over time, compression produces normalization of tight operation. What would have been perceived as constrained earlier becomes baseline expectation. The professional adapts behavior to narrow margin rather than restoring slack.

Adaptation stabilizes the compressed system temporarily but entrenches fragility.

The difference between hidden compression and acute shock becomes most visible during economic normalization.

In expansionary environments with suppressed volatility, compressed systems function smoothly. Income remains high. Variance appears minimal. Margin narrowing remains hidden because realized income consistently exceeds reliable floor.

When volatility returns to historical levels, income may revert toward dependable baseline. For preserved systems, this reversion reduces surplus but preserves commitments. For compressed systems, reversion collides with rigid load calibrated to peak income.

The result is not immediate insolvency. It is rapid compression escalation. The system moves from stable-but-brittle to strained within a short span because structural distance was already thin.

By the time visible instability appears, compression has been advancing for years.

Prevention requires decoupling growth from commitment scaling reflexively.

When reliable floor increases, margin should increase faster than rigidity. This requires resisting the efficiency narrative that slack is waste. Slack is structural insurance against inevitable variance.

Structural review must be quantitative, not intuitive. Reliable floor must be reassessed relative to current income variability. Rigid and semi-fixed load must be measured as a percentage of that floor. Duration stack must be evaluated for exposure across future cycles. Margin distance must be calculated explicitly.

If margin percentage declines despite income growth, compression is underway.

If margin percentage widens, tolerance is increasing.

Maintenance discipline is not restrictive. It enables controlled expansion. It ensures that growth produces resilience rather than fragility.

Margin compression is reversible but asymmetrical. It is easier to prevent narrowing than to restore distance once commitments are layered and durations extended.

Reversal may require forgoing new commitments during income growth until margin widens sufficiently. It may require pruning semi-fixed creep. It may require restructuring duration exposure when feasible. These actions are friction-heavy if deferred and lighter if performed early.

The central structural reality remains: tolerance depends on distance between dependable capacity and rigid load. Compression narrows that distance incrementally. Drift enables narrowing during prosperity. Stable-but-brittle systems emerge when visible performance masks declining tolerance.

Durable systems widen structural distance deliberately. They treat margin as core asset rather than idle surplus. They measure compression before instability forces correction.

Stability over long horizons is not the product of constant income growth. It is the product of preserved and expanded structural space within which income variability can occur without destabilization.

Compression has one further effect that becomes visible only when the system is observed under repeated decision cycles rather than under single financial events.

As margin narrows, the threshold for perceived disruption declines.

In a wide-margin system, a $5,000 unexpected expense relative to a $20,000 annual structural distance is material but not destabilizing. In a compressed system with $5,000 of structural distance remaining, the same expense consumes the entire buffer. The objective event is identical. The structural impact differs completely.

Because impact is experienced through structure, not magnitude alone, identical financial events produce different behavioral responses across architectures.

In preserved systems, unexpected costs are absorbed and evaluated within long-cycle context. In compressed systems, unexpected costs trigger immediate rebalancing. The rebalancing is often tactical and short-term—deferring allocations, shifting liquidity, sequencing payments with precision.

Repeated tactical rebalancing creates dependency on smooth inflow continuation. When income remains stable, the system can maintain near-limit operation. When income fluctuates, the absence of slack becomes visible.

Compression fatigue is not emotional burnout. It is structural exhaustion. The system operates close to constraint consistently. Each minor disturbance requires correction. Recovery velocity slows. Slack does not rebuild fully between cycles. Over time, the system remains in a semi-compressed state permanently.

Semi-compressed systems are particularly vulnerable to clustered variance.

Variance rarely occurs in isolation. Income may dip at the same time expenses rise. Timing misalignments may coincide with seasonal obligations. When margin is wide, clustering is manageable. When margin is narrow, clustering amplifies strain.

Clustering does not need to be severe to expose compression. It only needs to occur before full recovery from previous disturbance.

This is why hidden compression often reveals itself not during singular shocks but during ordinary sequences of moderate fluctuations.

Another structural consequence of prolonged compression is reduction in experimentation bandwidth.

Experimentation bandwidth is the range within which income can fluctuate temporarily without threatening core commitments. It defines how much short-term instability the system can tolerate in pursuit of long-term positioning.

In wide-margin architectures, experimentation bandwidth is substantial. Temporary reductions in income, transitional costs, or strategic investments can be absorbed. In compressed architectures, experimentation bandwidth approaches zero. Income must remain stable and near peak levels to preserve commitments.

This limitation reduces strategic flexibility across career cycles.

The professional may decline opportunities that involve short-term income variability because structural distance is insufficient. The architecture enforces continuity.

This enforcement is not ideological. It is mechanical. Rigid load calibrated near dependable capacity leaves no room for deviation.

Compression therefore reduces adaptability.

Adaptability is not luxury. It is necessary in environments where income structures evolve. Industries shift. Compensation models change. Market demand fluctuates. Systems that cannot adapt structurally to moderate shifts become dependent on static conditions.

Static conditions rarely persist across decades.

Prevention requires recognizing compression before it becomes binding.

The most reliable measurement is proportional rigidity: rigid and semi-fixed commitments as a percentage of reliable income floor. If this percentage trends upward, tolerance is declining regardless of income growth.

A secondary measurement is margin rebuild rate: how quickly structural distance returns to prior levels after moderate disturbance. If rebuild time lengthens, compression has advanced.

A third measurement is duration exposure concentration: the average maturity of fixed obligations relative to expected income stability horizon. If duration extends beyond volatility expectations without margin widening, risk accumulates.

A fourth measurement is discretionary contraction frequency: how often flexible categories must be reduced to protect baseline commitments. Increased frequency indicates narrowing elasticity.

These indicators are structural. They precede crisis. They are observable through deliberate review.

Income growth should first widen the gap between reliable floor and rigid load. Only after that gap is materially increased should new long-duration commitments be layered. Semi-fixed additions should be evaluated not only for monthly affordability but for cumulative density impact.

Margin is not merely a cushion for downturns. It is a design parameter that governs system behavior under normal variance.

Systems designed with visible structural distance respond to disturbance with contained adjustment. Systems designed with narrow structural distance respond with cascading adjustments.

The difference compounds over time.

When structural distance widens across cycles, resilience accumulates. When structural distance narrows across cycles, fragility accumulates.

The maintenance discipline required to prevent compression is straightforward in concept and demanding in execution.

Reliable floor must be recalculated periodically based on demonstrated income consistency. Rigid and semi-fixed commitments must be aggregated and measured against that floor. Duration layering must be mapped. Margin distance must be tracked explicitly rather than inferred from surplus.

If margin percentage declines, action is required before variance forces it.

Action may involve halting commitment expansion during income growth phases until structural distance widens. It may involve pruning semi-fixed creep. It may involve restructuring long-duration commitments when feasible. It may involve resisting efficiency narratives that equate full utilization with optimization.

Optimization in volatile systems requires slack.

Slack is not inefficiency. It is engineered resilience.

Without engineered resilience, systems rely on precision and favorable conditions to remain stable. Favorable conditions are cyclical. Precision is vulnerable to human and environmental variability.

Durable financial architecture requires deliberate preservation of measurable distance between dependable income and rigid obligation. Compression erodes that distance gradually. Drift normalizes erosion. Stability depends on interrupting that process before brittleness emerges.

Structural health is not defined by how much income flows through the system. It is defined by how much structural space exists within it.

There is an additional dimension to margin compression that emerges when observing systems across generational or multi-decade timelines rather than annual cycles.

Compression subtly alters the baseline from which each subsequent decision is made.

When margin is wide, the baseline includes structural slack. New commitments are layered onto a foundation that can absorb them. When margin is narrow, the baseline is already tight. Each new commitment is added onto constraint. Even if that commitment is small, it interacts with a compressed architecture.

Over time, compressed baselines compound constraint because each decision is evaluated relative to minimal slack rather than to meaningful structural distance.

This produces a ratcheting effect.

In expansionary periods, income growth permits incremental commitment expansion. Slack is quickly converted into rigidity. In plateau periods, rigidity remains while slack does not expand. When contraction occurs, slack is insufficient to absorb it, and reactive contraction is required. After contraction, slack may be restored partially but rarely to its original width because commitments have long durations.

Thus the system oscillates around a progressively narrower margin unless disciplined intervention occurs.

The ratchet operates asymmetrically. It is easy to increase rigidity during prosperity. It is friction-heavy to decrease rigidity during contraction. Transaction costs, renegotiation barriers, asset illiquidity, and identity factors increase the cost of reversal. As a result, rigidity growth often outpaces rigidity reduction across cycles.

Without explicit maintenance, compression becomes path-dependent.

Path dependence means that early prosperity decisions shape structural capacity decades later. Long-duration commitments layered during income peaks remain binding during income normalization. Semi-fixed creep accumulated during stable periods remains embedded when volatility widens.

Because commitments outlive the conditions under which they were justified, compression accumulates invisibly across macro cycles.

Another compounding mechanism appears through interaction with inflation and nominal income growth.

Nominal income may increase gradually over time, creating perception of expanding capacity. If rigid commitments increase proportionally or slightly faster, real structural distance does not expand. Inflation-adjusted reliable floor may stagnate relative to real rigid load. The system appears to grow in nominal terms while margin remains static or declines in real terms.

This illusion of growth can mask compression for extended periods.

Structural distance must be measured relative to dependable capacity, not relative to nominal earnings alone. If the percentage of reliable income consumed by rigidity trends upward, compression is occurring regardless of nominal growth.

A compressed system operating under nominal growth may appear prosperous externally while experiencing declining internal tolerance.

Over long horizons, the absence of widening margin limits capital allocation flexibility.

When margin is preserved and widened, excess capacity can be directed toward strengthening the system—building liquidity buffers, investing in durable assets, or increasing future dependable income streams. When margin is compressed, excess capacity is scarce. Surplus is minimal. Investment decisions are constrained by liquidity needs tied to rigid commitments.

This constraint reduces the ability to transform income growth into structural improvement.

Compressed systems often become consumption-scaled rather than resilience-scaled. Income growth fuels lifestyle scaling rather than structural strengthening.

In contrast, preserved systems convert income growth into increased resilience first and lifestyle scaling second. Over decades, this sequencing produces significant divergence in stability under stress.

The divergence becomes most visible during structural transitions: industry disruption, technological change, health events, or family restructuring.

In compressed architectures, such transitions may require immediate and substantial contraction of commitments or rapid income restoration.

In preserved architectures, transitions can be navigated within existing margin without destabilizing baseline.

The mechanical distinction is not income magnitude but structural distance.

Compression also increases reliance on stable macro conditions. When margin is narrow, the system implicitly depends on low volatility, stable employment conditions, and predictable revenue cycles. If external volatility increases, the architecture is not positioned to absorb it.

In this way, compression embeds macro dependence into micro structure.

Conversely, preserved-margin systems are less dependent on specific macro conditions because structural slack absorbs moderate volatility without cascading effects.

This macro insulation is a structural advantage, not a speculative one.

Early detection remains the only efficient defense.

When rigidity as a percentage of reliable floor rises persistently, compression is advancing.

When discretionary flexibility declines in frequency and magnitude, elasticity is narrowing.

When contract stack duration extends into time horizons longer than demonstrated income stability, exposure is rising.

When recovery from moderate disturbances slows across cycles, margin is insufficient.

When planning horizons shrink because near-term cash impact dominates evaluation, compression has already altered behavior.

These are measurable, mechanical indicators.

Reliable income growth must outpace rigidity growth. Semi-fixed creep must be reversed deliberately rather than tolerated. Duration layering must be constrained relative to dependable capacity. New commitments must be evaluated not only for affordability but for effect on proportional rigidity and margin distance.

Slack must be reintroduced intentionally.

Slack, when reintroduced, alters system dynamics immediately. Variance propagation slows. Recovery velocity increases. Sequencing sensitivity declines. Liquidity substitution becomes unnecessary. Cognitive load decreases. Planning horizon extends.

These effects confirm that margin is the primary determinant of tolerance.

Margin compression is not a moral failing or a budgeting error. It is a structural outcome of unmeasured growth interacting with incremental commitment layering.

Structural drift is the default in prosperous environments. Without deliberate countermeasures, slack is converted into obligation reflexively.

Durability requires resisting reflex.

Income magnitude alone does not create stability. Structural distance does.

A system that widens structural distance across cycles will strengthen even if income growth is modest. A system that narrows structural distance during income growth will weaken even if income is high.

Over decades, this divergence determines whether financial architecture remains adaptable or becomes brittle.

The objective is not to minimize commitments but to maintain measurable space between dependable income and committed load.

When that space is visible and preserved, the system retains tolerance under variance. When that space narrows unnoticed, stability becomes conditional.

Margin compression is the silent erosion of tolerance. Structural drift is the process that enables it. Maintenance discipline is the mechanism that prevents it.

Durable financial control depends on preserving structural distance as intentionally as income is pursued.

The final structural consequence of sustained margin compression is that it changes the system's equilibrium point.

In preserved architectures, equilibrium exists at a position of slack. The system naturally stabilizes with structural distance between dependable capacity and rigid load. Surplus is not fully converted into obligation. Variance is absorbed without altering baseline configuration. The resting state includes tolerance.

In compressed architectures, equilibrium shifts toward full utilization. The system stabilizes near its dependable ceiling. Surplus is quickly translated into obligation. Baseline commitments expand to occupy available capacity. The resting state includes minimal slack.

This shift in equilibrium is gradual. It occurs through repeated decisions that convert temporary capacity into permanent load. Once equilibrium shifts, it becomes self-reinforcing.

When slack exists, new commitments are evaluated against preservation of that slack. When slack does not exist, new commitments are evaluated against immediate feasibility. The evaluation framework itself changes.

Over time, the compressed equilibrium produces structural inertia.

Structural inertia is the resistance to change caused by high rigidity density and long duration exposure. Even if income grows meaningfully, inertia prevents rapid widening of margin because commitments absorb growth reflexively. Even if income contracts moderately, inertia prevents rapid contraction of rigidity because commitments are locked.

The system becomes slow-moving in both directions.

Slow-moving systems are vulnerable in environments characterized by variability. They cannot expand margin quickly in growth phases because commitments scale. They cannot contract commitments quickly in contraction phases because duration exposure locks them in.

The result is oscillation around narrow tolerance bands.

Oscillation is expensive. Each contraction requires defensive adjustment. Each expansion invites renewed compression. Over decades, the cumulative cost of oscillation—transactional, strategic, cognitive—exceeds the cost of preserving slack during growth.

Preserved systems avoid oscillation because margin widens in growth phases and remains sufficient in contraction phases. Equilibrium is centered around structural distance rather than around full utilization.

Compression also alters intertemporal trade-offs.

In wide-margin systems, decisions can be evaluated over multi-cycle horizons. Temporary inefficiencies may be tolerated if they produce long-term structural improvement. In compressed systems, short-term cash impact dominates. Multi-cycle optimization becomes secondary to immediate stabilization.

This shift reduces the system's ability to invest in durable capacity.

Durable capacity includes education, business development, geographic mobility, and asset acquisition aligned with long-term reliability. When margin is narrow, such investments must be weighed against immediate rigidity obligations. Many are deferred or abandoned.

Deferred structural improvement compounds fragility. Income structure may stagnate. Reliable floor may not rise meaningfully. Yet rigidity remains. Margin does not widen. Compression persists.

The system becomes optimized for continuity, not for durability.

Another mechanical effect of compression is reduced error tolerance.

In preserved architectures, minor errors—administrative mistakes, billing discrepancies, misestimation of expenses—are absorbed without structural consequence. In compressed architectures, minor errors can propagate into temporary instability because slack is minimal.

Reduced error tolerance increases operational vigilance. Monitoring intensifies. Administrative precision becomes essential. While precision is beneficial, reliance on precision as primary stabilizer indicates structural fragility.

Precision is a behavioral patch. Margin is a structural solution.

Over extended periods, reliance on behavioral precision to maintain stability increases cognitive load. The professional must continually manage inflow timing, outflow scheduling, and liquidity allocation to avoid compression tipping into instability.

Cognitive load is a real cost. It consumes bandwidth that could be deployed toward growth, strategy, or innovation.

Preserved systems offload much of this cognitive burden to structure. Slack absorbs variability automatically. Monitoring remains important but is not central to survival.

The difference between structural resilience and behavioral vigilance becomes increasingly important as complexity grows.

As careers advance, income structures diversify, tax complexity increases, and obligations multiply. Compressed systems struggle under complexity because each additional variable interacts with narrow margin. Preserved systems integrate complexity more smoothly because slack buffers interactions.

Complexity without slack magnifies fragility.

Therefore, margin compression not only narrows tolerance; it amplifies the destabilizing effect of complexity.

Maintenance discipline must account for complexity growth.

Periodic structural review should not only measure rigidity percentage and margin distance but also assess whether system complexity has increased without proportional slack expansion. If complexity increases while margin remains constant or declines, fragility increases nonlinearly.

In long-cycle perspective, the objective is to maintain equilibrium at a position of structural slack rather than at full utilization.

Full utilization appears efficient in static analysis. In dynamic environments, it is brittle.

Slack, properly calibrated, is not excess. It is capacity reserved for inevitable variability.

Growth that does not increase slack increases exposure. Growth that increases slack increases resilience.

Structural distance must be treated as primary output of financial architecture.

If income grows and structural distance grows faster, the system strengthens. If income grows and structural distance grows slower or declines, the system weakens relative to volatility.

Margin compression is the narrowing of that structural distance. Structural drift is the incremental process that enables narrowing. Prosperity accelerates drift by suppressing visible volatility and encouraging utilization of slack.

Durable systems interrupt drift intentionally. They widen margin before scaling commitments. They measure rigidity relative to dependable capacity rather than relative to nominal income. They review duration layering before extending exposure. They treat semi-fixed creep as structural load rather than as trivial expense.

These practices maintain equilibrium around slack rather than around constraint.

In unstable environments, stability does not arise from maximizing income or minimizing spending alone. It arises from preserving sufficient structural space between dependable capacity and committed load so that ordinary variance does not require structural reaction.

When that space is protected and expanded deliberately, the system remains tolerant under fluctuation. When that space erodes gradually, stability becomes conditional on continued favorable conditions.

Margin compression is the quiet migration from tolerance to conditional stability.

Structural discipline determines whether that migration continues or is reversed.

Compression also reshapes the way feedback is interpreted inside the system.

In a wide-margin architecture, feedback from minor disturbances is informative but not destabilizing. A modest income dip signals volatility within expected bands. An expense overrun signals need for adjustment. The signal can be processed calmly because structural distance remains intact.

In a compressed architecture, identical signals are amplified. Because slack is minimal, each disturbance interacts immediately with rigid load. The signal feels urgent because it is structurally urgent. The system cannot ignore it. Feedback loops accelerate.

Accelerated feedback loops increase reactivity. Decisions are made to protect near-term solvency rather than to optimize long-term configuration. Tactical balancing becomes habitual.

When tactical balancing becomes routine, structural review often recedes. The system is busy maintaining equilibrium at a compressed level. Attention shifts from architecture to execution. Execution replaces design.

Over time, this substitution reduces the likelihood of deliberate margin widening because operational demands consume capacity for structural recalibration.

The structural consequence is independent of motivation. When slack is converted into rigidity, tolerance declines mechanically.

A preserved system may appear conservative in visible consumption terms while accumulating structural strength invisibly. A compressed system may appear optimized and successful while narrowing tolerance invisibly.

Only under variance does the difference become apparent.

Variance exposure tests equilibrium point.

In preserved systems, moderate income contraction or expense clustering leaves core commitments unaffected. In compressed systems, moderate contraction forces structural response because rigid load is calibrated near dependable capacity.

The response may not be dramatic. It may involve reducing discretionary categories, postponing savings contributions, or increasing liquidity substitution. But the presence of required response indicates insufficient margin.

Repeated required responses indicate compression.

Over long horizons, required responses accumulate friction.

Friction includes administrative burden, strategic constraint, opportunity cost, and cognitive strain. These costs rarely appear in balance sheets but materially affect system durability.

In contrast, preserved systems require fewer reactive adjustments. Friction is lower. Recovery velocity is higher. Cognitive bandwidth remains available for growth.

Structural maintenance is therefore not about eliminating variance but about minimizing friction under variance.

Margin widening reduces friction per disturbance. Compression increases friction per disturbance.

Over decades, the cumulative difference in friction is substantial.

Early in career, optionality horizon is long. There is time to recover from structural missteps. As career progresses, optionality horizon shortens. Recovery windows narrow. Long-duration commitments extend into later life stages. Compression in mid-career may become more consequential later because duration exposure intersects with reduced income flexibility.

If margin is preserved early and widened across cycles, later-life volatility is less destabilizing. If compression accumulates early and persists, later-life volatility intersects with rigid commitments that are difficult to unwind.

Structural foresight requires anticipating that volatility is not confined to early career.

Maintenance discipline must therefore persist across life stages. Income growth at any stage should first widen structural distance. Duration layering should be evaluated relative to long-term volatility expectations, not only to current income stability.

The prevention principle remains consistent: growth must widen tolerance before scaling commitments.

When this principle is followed consistently, structural distance expands across cycles. The system's equilibrium shifts toward slack rather than toward constraint. Variance remains contained.

When this principle is ignored, structural distance erodes gradually. The system's equilibrium shifts toward full utilization. Variance propagates quickly.

Structural drift is the default trajectory of systems experiencing prosperity without measurement. Maintenance discipline is the counterforce.

Reliable floor must be recalculated periodically. Rigid and semi-fixed load must be aggregated explicitly. Duration stack must be mapped. Margin distance must be measured as proportion of dependable capacity. Scenario testing under moderate variance must confirm that commitments remain insulated.

If these reviews indicate narrowing structural distance, corrective action must precede visible instability.

Correction is always more efficient when performed early. Pruning semi-fixed creep when density is moderate is simpler than unwinding layered commitments when density is high. Allowing income growth to accumulate as slack for multiple cycles is easier than rebuilding slack after contraction.

Structural distance is easier to preserve than to restore.

The chapter reaches its structural close here: margin compression is the gradual erosion of tolerance through incremental rigidity growth relative to dependable capacity. It can occur during prosperity. It can coexist with rising income. It becomes visible only under variance. Durable financial architecture depends on making structural distance explicit, measuring it consistently, and widening it deliberately across growth cycles.

Liquidity Architecture and Runway Design

Liquidity is frequently described as cash availability. Structurally, it is time.

Liquidity converts income capacity into duration of survivable variance. It determines how long obligations can be met when inflow deviates from expectation. Margin defines structural distance in magnitude. Liquidity defines structural distance in time.

This distinction is foundational.

Liquidity as buffer is static capacity. It represents stored resources that can absorb temporary mismatch between inflow and outflow. Liquidity as flow is dynamic capacity. It represents the ongoing movement of income through the system that maintains equilibrium. Both matter, but they function differently.

A system may exhibit strong income flow and weak buffer liquidity. Under stable conditions, the flow sustains obligations. Under disruption, absence of buffer compresses tolerance quickly. Conversely, a system may hold substantial liquidity reserves but operate with fragile structural configuration, creating ongoing compression despite visible cash balances.

Liquidity must therefore be integrated into architecture rather than treated as an isolated metric.

The structure of liquidity is tiered.

Operational liquidity exists to manage routine sequencing mismatches. It absorbs minor timing differences between inflow and outflow. It ensures that obligations due within a cycle can be satisfied without tactical maneuvering. Operational liquidity is short-duration and frequently accessed. It prevents timing friction from escalating into structural strain.

Tactical liquidity exists to absorb moderate income deviation or clustered expense events. It spans multiple cycles. Tactical reserves provide room for income dips, delayed payments, or concentrated obligations without requiring commitment reduction. Tactical liquidity bridges variance that is temporary but material.

Strategic liquidity exists to support structural transitions or prolonged variance. It enables sustained operation below normal income levels while preserving core commitments. Strategic reserves are not intended for routine use. They define runway.

Runway is a time-based tolerance metric. It measures how many cycles the system can operate if income declines to a defined stress level while rigid commitments remain intact.

Runway is not an arbitrary number of months. It is the translation of liquidity into duration relative to reliable floor and rigid load.

If reliable monthly income floor is $12,000 and rigid commitments are $8,000, margin in magnitude terms is $4,000. If tactical and strategic liquidity combined equal $24,000, runway under complete income loss would approximate three months of rigid coverage. Under partial income contraction to reliable floor, runway extends further because some inflow continues.

Runway depends on scenario definition.

Under moderate contraction—income declining 20 percent below reliable floor—liquidity supplements reduced margin rather than replacing full income. Under severe contraction, liquidity becomes primary support. The structural objective is not elimination of income volatility but provision of sufficient time to respond without destabilizing commitments.

Time expands choice.

Without runway, income contraction requires immediate structural adjustment. With runway, income contraction can be evaluated and responded to deliberately.

Liquidity decay under compression is common.

As margin narrows, surplus available for liquidity accumulation declines. Semi-fixed creep and duration layering consume dependable capacity. Tactical reserves are drawn more frequently for minor disturbances. Strategic reserves may be partially repurposed to maintain baseline during compressed cycles.

Over time, liquidity buffers erode even while income remains high.

Decay can occur without explicit depletion. If income grows but liquidity does not grow proportionally relative to rigid load, effective runway shortens. Liquidity must be measured relative to committed obligations, not in nominal isolation.

For example, a professional with $60,000 in liquid reserves and $5,000 in monthly rigid commitments holds twelve months of coverage. If rigid commitments expand to $8,000 monthly without increasing reserves, runway shrinks to seven and a half months despite identical cash balance.

Liquidity adequacy is proportional to rigidity density.

Sequencing risk interacts with liquidity architecture.

Sequencing risk is the exposure created by timing mismatch between inflow and outflow. Even with adequate annual income and sufficient margin, misaligned timing can create short-term compression. Operational liquidity absorbs such mismatches. Without operational liquidity, minor timing shifts require tactical or strategic reserve deployment unnecessarily.

When operational liquidity is insufficient, the system escalates to higher tiers prematurely. Tactical reserves intended for moderate variance are consumed by routine sequencing friction. Strategic reserves intended for prolonged variance are touched for operational imbalance.

This tier collapse reduces runway invisibly.

Liquidity substitution differs from structural margin.

Margin absorbs magnitude variance. Liquidity absorbs time variance. When margin is wide, liquidity use is minimal under moderate contraction because surplus remains available. When margin is narrow, liquidity substitutes for absent structural distance. Tactical reserves are used to maintain commitments that exceed dependable income.

Liquidity substitution can mask compression temporarily. Obligations remain current. The system appears stable. Yet reliance on reserves to sustain baseline indicates structural misalignment.

Repeated liquidity substitution shortens runway and increases vulnerability to extended variance.

Over-liquidity inefficiency and under-liquidity fragility represent opposing miscalibrations.

Excess liquidity relative to volatility band and rigidity profile may impose opportunity cost. Idle cash beyond reasonable runway duration reduces capacity for productive allocation. However, inefficiency must be evaluated relative to volatility and duration exposure. What appears excessive under stable conditions may be appropriate under wider variance expectations.

Under-liquidity fragility is structurally more dangerous. Insufficient operational liquidity increases sequencing sensitivity. Insufficient tactical liquidity reduces ability to absorb moderate contraction. Insufficient strategic liquidity eliminates runway for transition or prolonged variance.

Calibration of liquidity must reference volatility band, rigidity density, and duration exposure simultaneously.

A professional with narrow volatility band and low rigidity density requires less runway than one with wide volatility band and high long-duration commitments. Liquidity architecture is not universal; it is configuration-dependent.

Liquidity as autonomy amplifier becomes evident during variance.

When liquidity tiers are calibrated properly, income disruption does not immediately constrain decision-making. Tactical reserves provide breathing room. Strategic reserves allow evaluation of alternatives. Autonomy persists because time is available.

Without liquidity runway, even moderate income disruption forces rapid adjustment. Commitments must be renegotiated or reduced quickly. Professional options narrow because structural time buffer is absent.

Time buffer equals autonomy.

Liquidity maintenance discipline parallels margin maintenance discipline.

Operational liquidity must be replenished routinely to absorb sequencing mismatch. Tactical reserves must be rebuilt after moderate disturbance. Strategic reserves must remain insulated from routine use.

Periodic review should calculate runway under defined stress scenarios. Rigid commitments must be compared against available liquidity to determine duration of survivability without structural adjustment.

If runway shortens due to rigidity growth or reserve decay, corrective action must precede variance exposure.

Liquidity architecture complements margin architecture. Margin absorbs magnitude deviation. Liquidity absorbs duration deviation. Both must be calibrated relative to reliable floor and rigidity profile.

When liquidity is structured tier-wise and measured against time-based tolerance, the system gains resilience under both short-term timing mismatch and medium-term income contraction.

When liquidity is unstructured or under-calibrated, variance propagates quickly from timing friction into structural instability.

Liquidity is not merely stored cash. It is the time dimension of financial stability.

Liquidity architecture becomes meaningful only when modeled under variance rather than under steady-state flow.

Under stable conditions, income flow sustains obligations, and operational liquidity absorbs minor timing mismatches. Tactical and strategic tiers remain untouched. The system appears simple. Cash accumulates, obligations are met, and reserves may appear excessive.

Under variance, the distinctions between tiers become operationally significant.

Consider moderate income contraction relative to reliable floor. If inflow declines by fifteen to twenty percent for several cycles, margin in magnitude terms shrinks. If margin remains positive, obligations continue to be met without reserve use. Liquidity remains intact.

If contraction exceeds margin, tactical liquidity activates. Tactical reserves bridge the gap between reduced inflow and rigid commitments. The system continues operating without renegotiation of commitments. Strategic reserves remain insulated.

If contraction persists beyond tactical horizon, strategic liquidity defines runway. Strategic reserves determine how many cycles the system can operate below reliable floor without altering rigid load.

The interaction between margin and liquidity is sequential. Margin absorbs first. Tactical liquidity absorbs next. Strategic liquidity absorbs prolonged deviation. If all three are insufficient, structural reconfiguration becomes necessary.

Compression alters this sequence.

When margin has narrowed due to structural drift, even modest contraction bypasses margin and activates liquidity tiers prematurely. Tactical reserves are drawn more frequently. Strategic reserves may be accessed for events that would not have required them in preserved architectures.

This premature activation accelerates liquidity decay.

Liquidity decay does not require severe crisis. It can occur through repeated moderate reserve use without full replenishment. If income rebounds only partially before next disturbance, reserves may not return to prior levels. Over time, runway shortens even if nominal income remains strong.

Runway must therefore be measured dynamically, not assumed static because of prior accumulation.

Sequencing risk interacts with liquidity at the operational tier.

If inflow timing shifts by days or weeks while rigid obligations remain fixed, operational liquidity must be sufficient to prevent tactical reserve drawdown. When operational liquidity is thin, tactical reserves become de facto operational buffers. This degrades tier separation.

Tier separation is critical because each tier serves different duration horizons. Collapsing tiers reduces system clarity. Tactical reserves intended for moderate contraction become consumed by routine mismatch. Strategic reserves intended for structural transition are eroded by operational friction.

Maintaining tier separation preserves runway integrity.

Liquidity substitution differs from margin expansion.

When structural margin is insufficient to cover rigid load under moderate contraction, liquidity substitutes temporarily. Substitution is viable only if reserves are adequate and contraction is temporary. If substitution becomes recurrent, structural misalignment persists.

Repeated substitution without margin correction reduces autonomy. Each reserve draw reduces future optionality. The system becomes dependent on restoration of favorable inflow rather than on structural adjustment.

Over time, reliance on liquidity substitution can mask compression. Because obligations remain current, the system appears stable. Yet runway shortens silently.

Liquidity must be evaluated relative to volatility band and rigidity density.

A professional with narrow income variance and low rigidity density may require modest tactical reserves because margin absorbs most moderate deviation. Strategic reserves can be calibrated conservatively.

A professional with wide income variance and high rigidity density requires deeper tactical reserves and more substantial strategic runway because margin alone cannot absorb moderate contraction.

Calibration is proportional.

Liquidity as autonomy amplifier becomes visible during transitional periods.

If a professional contemplates a role change involving temporary income reduction, strategic liquidity determines feasibility without immediate commitment reduction. If strategic reserves cover multiple cycles of reduced inflow, transition can occur deliberately. If reserves are thin, transition may be deferred despite long-term benefit.

Liquidity transforms variance from threat into negotiable condition.

Autonomy is not defined by income magnitude alone. It is defined by the time buffer available under deviation.

Over-liquidity inefficiency is sometimes cited as justification for minimal reserves. Idle cash may appear underutilized compared to potential investment returns. However, efficiency must be evaluated relative to system volatility.

If volatility band is wide and rigidity density high, substantial liquidity is structurally rational. The opportunity cost of idle cash must be compared against the friction and risk of insufficient runway during contraction.

Under-liquidity fragility is more consequential than moderate over-liquidity inefficiency.

Insufficient liquidity forces rapid structural reaction to moderate deviation. It increases reliance on precision and favorable timing. It compresses planning horizon. It reduces optionality.

Optimal calibration lies between idle excess and fragile scarcity. That calibration depends on volatility, rigidity, and duration exposure.

Liquidity maintenance discipline parallels margin maintenance.

Operational tier must remain adequate for sequencing mismatches. Tactical tier must be rebuilt after moderate use before new commitments are layered. Strategic tier must be insulated from routine draws and replenished deliberately if accessed.

Periodic runway analysis should test multiple stress levels: moderate contraction, severe contraction, and clustered variance. If runway under moderate contraction is measured in weeks rather than months, liquidity is insufficient relative to structure.

Liquidity architecture is not static. As rigidity grows or reliable floor shifts, liquidity tiers must adjust proportionally. If rigid load increases, runway shortens unless reserves grow. If volatility widens, deeper tactical buffers are required.

Conversely, if rigidity declines and volatility narrows, liquidity requirements may be recalibrated downward without reducing tolerance.

The structural objective is time-based tolerance aligned with magnitude-based margin.

Margin absorbs immediate magnitude mismatch. Liquidity absorbs duration mismatch. When both are calibrated relative to dependable capacity and volatility expectation, the system remains stable under ordinary and moderate variance.

When liquidity is thin relative to rigidity and volatility, variance accelerates into structural strain rapidly. When liquidity is deep relative to configuration, variance remains contained.

Liquidity is therefore not a secondary consideration after income and obligations. It is co-equal with margin in defining tolerance.

Margin defines how much deviation can occur in a cycle without strain. Liquidity defines how long deviation can persist without reconfiguration.

Time and magnitude form the two axes of financial durability.

When both axes are intentionally designed and maintained, stability persists even in unstable environments.

Liquidity architecture also determines how the system behaves under asymmetric variance.

Income disruptions are rarely uniform. They may be sudden and deep, gradual and prolonged, or intermittent and clustered. Each pattern interacts differently with margin and runway.

A sudden and deep income interruption tests strategic liquidity immediately. If income falls sharply below reliable floor for a single cycle but recovers quickly, tactical reserves may be sufficient. If the interruption extends beyond tactical horizon, strategic reserves determine survival duration without altering rigid commitments.

A gradual and prolonged income decline tests margin first and liquidity second. Margin absorbs early deviation. Tactical liquidity sustains mid-phase deviation. Strategic liquidity supports later phases. If reserves are shallow relative to duration of contraction, structural adjustment becomes unavoidable.

Intermittent clustered variance tests operational and tactical tiers simultaneously. If income dips occur repeatedly before reserves are rebuilt, runway erodes incrementally. The system may never face dramatic shock yet progressively lose tolerance.

Liquidity must therefore be robust to pattern, not merely to magnitude.

Runway design requires explicit stress modeling.

The relevant question is not how much cash is available in isolation, but how many cycles of rigid commitment coverage exist under defined income stress conditions. If reliable floor is $15,000 monthly and rigid load is $10,000, and if strategic reserves equal $60,000, runway under zero income is six months. Under partial income contraction to $7,500 monthly, runway extends further because inflow continues.

These distinctions matter because most variance is partial, not absolute.

Calibration must also consider refill dynamics.

If liquidity is drawn during moderate contraction and income rebounds, reserves must be rebuilt before new commitments are added.

Failure to rebuild preserves compressed runway. Income recovery without liquidity restoration creates illusion of restored stability while time buffer remains thin.

Refill discipline prevents runway erosion.

Liquidity architecture interacts with rigidity density in nonlinear ways.

At low rigidity density, modest liquidity provides substantial runway because monthly obligations are limited. At high rigidity density, identical liquidity provides shorter runway because obligations consume greater share of reserves per cycle.

Thus, as rigidity density increases, liquidity requirements rise disproportionately if tolerance is to remain constant.

Duration layering intensifies this relationship.

When long-term commitments extend over decades, liquidity must cover not only short-term volatility but also the probability of cyclical contraction occurring within those durations. A thirty-year obligation increases likelihood that multiple volatility phases will occur before maturity. Liquidity buffers must be sufficient to bridge those phases without forcing structural breach.

Short-duration commitments allow recalibration before extended volatility accumulates. Long-duration commitments require deeper runway.

Liquidity substitution under compression must be distinguished from planned reserve deployment.

Planned deployment occurs when reserves are intentionally used for defined transitional objectives with rebuild strategy in place. Substitution under compression occurs when reserves are used to sustain baseline that exceeds dependable capacity, without structural correction.

Substitution can temporarily preserve appearance of stability while silently shortening runway. If substitution becomes habitual, strategic liquidity transforms into operational support, collapsing tier separation.

Tier collapse increases fragility because reserves intended for extended variance are consumed by routine shortfalls.

Over-liquidity inefficiency should be evaluated in context of volatility and rigidity, not in abstract terms of return optimization.

Holding twelve months of strategic runway in a system with high income volatility and long-duration commitments may be structurally rational even if nominal returns on liquidity are low. Conversely, holding equivalent reserves in a system with stable salary and low rigidity density may exceed necessary tolerance.

Calibration is system-specific.

Liquidity as autonomy amplifier becomes most visible during opportunity windows.

A professional considering a business launch, geographic relocation, or strategic sabbatical can evaluate feasibility objectively only if runway exists. Without runway, even high income may not translate into freedom because obligations consume dependable capacity immediately.

Liquidity provides decision time.

Decision time reduces forced outcomes. Without decision time, choices are constrained by urgency rather than by optimization.

Liquidity maintenance discipline requires separation of tiers operationally and psychologically.

Operational balances should not be conflated with tactical reserves. Tactical reserves should not be conflated with strategic runway. Each tier must have defined purpose and threshold.

Periodic review must calculate runway under multiple stress scenarios and compare against duration exposure and volatility expectations. If runway under moderate contraction falls below acceptable horizon, corrective action must precede new rigidity.

Corrective action may involve rebuilding reserves through surplus retention, moderating new commitments, or adjusting duration exposure where feasible.

Liquidity architecture is dynamic.

As reliable floor grows and margin widens, liquidity requirements may adjust. As volatility widens or rigidity density increases, liquidity tiers must deepen proportionally. Static reserve targets independent of system configuration produce miscalibration.

The objective is not maximum liquidity. It is sufficient time-based tolerance aligned with magnitude-based structure.

When liquidity and margin are both calibrated intentionally, the system withstands both magnitude shocks and duration shocks. When margin is wide but liquidity thin, prolonged variance can destabilize otherwise sound architecture. When liquidity is deep but margin narrow, repeated moderate shocks may drain reserves unnecessarily.

Balance between time and magnitude axes defines durability.

Liquidity is therefore not secondary to structural configuration. It is the temporal complement.

Runway design converts abstract financial strength into measurable survival horizon. It transforms uncertainty into manageable interval.

When runway is adequate, variance does not dictate immediate reaction. When runway is inadequate, even modest deviation compresses options.

Liquidity architecture determines whether time is ally or adversary under volatility.

Exposure Concentration and Income Fragility

Income concentration is a structural exposure variable, not a career descriptor. It measures the degree to which dependable capacity relies on a single inflow source or on multiple sources that behave similarly under variance. When reliable income floor is derived primarily from one employer, one dominant client, one product channel, or one compensation structure, the system inherits the variance characteristics of that source.

Concentration does not imply instability under normal conditions. A single employer with long tenure and consistent compensation may produce narrow short-term volatility. Concentration becomes structural fragility when variance at the source propagates directly to the entire income base.

If reliable floor is supported by one inflow and that inflow contracts materially, there is no internal diversification to dampen the effect. Margin and liquidity may absorb the shock temporarily, but exposure concentration determines magnitude of initial impact.

Revenue stream correlation amplifies this fragility.

Multiple income streams do not necessarily reduce exposure if they are correlated. Two clients in the same industry, two product lines dependent on the same demand cycle, salary and bonus tied to identical company performance metrics—these are nominally diversified inflows but structurally linked. When underlying driver contracts, both streams decline simultaneously.

Correlation transforms apparent diversification into effective concentration.

Under stable macro conditions, correlated revenue streams may reinforce growth. Under contraction, they amplify decline. The system behaves as if dependent on a single source.

Fixed-cost coupling intensifies concentrated exposure.

When rigid commitments are calibrated relative to reliable floor derived from a concentrated inflow, obligations implicitly assume continuity of that source. If fixed and semi-fixed load is proportionate to dependable income during stable periods but the dependable income itself is highly concentrated, structural fragility exists despite disciplined margin management.

For example, a professional may maintain appropriate margin relative to salary, yet if salary represents nearly all dependable capacity and is tied to one firm's performance, exposure is high. Margin absorbs moderate fluctuation. It cannot offset structural loss of inflow beyond its capacity.

Concentration versus diversification presents a trade-off between efficiency and resilience.

Concentration can increase efficiency. Specialization within one employer or channel may maximize compensation growth. Focus can deepen expertise and increase income magnitude. Administrative simplicity reduces friction. Diversification introduces complexity, coordination cost, and potential dilution of focus.

Resilience requires some degree of decoupling. Diversification spreads exposure across independent drivers. It reduces magnitude of variance transmitted to the system when any single driver contracts.

The structural objective is not maximal fragmentation of income streams. Excess fragmentation can reduce efficiency and increase operational complexity. The objective is proportional exposure—alignment between concentration level and system tolerance.

Hidden exposure stacking frequently undermines apparent stability.

Equity compensation tied to employer performance, bonuses contingent on company profitability, retirement contributions linked to stock value, and industry clustering of both employment and investments create layered exposure to a single macro driver.

A professional employed in a technology firm, compensated partly in equity, invested heavily in technology sector funds, and residing in a geography economically dependent on that sector may appear diversified by asset class and income category. Structurally, exposure is stacked along one industry axis.

Under expansion, stacking accelerates wealth accumulation. Under contraction, stacking amplifies loss of both income and asset value simultaneously. Margin and liquidity must absorb compounded shocks.

Professional identity lock-in compounds income concentration.

When skills, credentials, and networks are tightly coupled to one employer or industry, adaptability declines. Income becomes rigid not only because of contract structure but because mobility options narrow. The professional's reliable floor is tied to continuity within a specific ecosystem.

Lock-in increases fragility because external variance affecting that ecosystem directly threatens dependable capacity. Even if alternative roles exist, transition friction may be high due to specialization.

Structural decoupling requires income layering without excessive fragmentation.

Layering does not require equal weighting across multiple sources. It requires partial independence of drivers. A secondary income stream in a different industry, advisory work not tied to employer performance, or product revenue unrelated to primary channel can introduce uncorrelated inflow.

The objective is not symmetry but offset potential. When primary inflow contracts, secondary inflow remains stable or declines less severely.

Over-fragmentation introduces administrative burden and may dilute primary income growth. Under-fragmentation leaves the system vulnerable to concentrated shock. Proportional exposure balances these forces.

Proportional exposure as a stability principle means that concentration should be calibrated relative to margin and liquidity architecture.

High concentration requires wider margin and deeper liquidity to compensate. Lower concentration allows similar tolerance with narrower buffers because income shocks are less likely to eliminate entire dependable capacity simultaneously.

Income fragility under macro reversion becomes most visible when concentrated exposure intersects with industry-wide contraction.

During expansionary cycles, concentration may appear safe because volatility is low. When macro conditions revert, correlated revenue streams contract together. Salary may freeze or decline. Bonuses may disappear. Equity value may fall. Secondary income tied to same sector may shrink.

If rigid commitments were calibrated to peak income under suppressed volatility, compression accelerates. Liquidity tiers activate quickly. Runway shortens.

In diversified architectures, contraction in one stream may be partially offset by stability in another. The system absorbs shock with less severe activation of liquidity reserves.

Configuration redesign under concentrated exposure involves rebalancing inflow sources relative to structural tolerance.

If primary income source remains highly concentrated, margin and liquidity must widen proportionally. If margin widening is impractical, secondary income layering must introduce partial decoupling. If neither occurs, rigid commitments must remain conservative relative to reliable floor to preserve tolerance.

The structural objective is not elimination of concentration but alignment between exposure profile and tolerance capacity.

A highly concentrated income structure can be stable if margin is wide, liquidity runway is deep, and rigid load is proportionate. A diversified income structure can still be fragile if correlated drivers exist and rigid commitments are excessive.

Exposure concentration is therefore not inherently negative. It is a multiplier. It magnifies both growth and contraction. Architecture must absorb that amplification.

Income fragility emerges when concentration, rigidity density, and insufficient liquidity intersect.

Under stable conditions, fragility remains hidden. Under variance, amplification reveals it.

Stability in unstable environments requires conscious calibration of exposure concentration relative to structural buffers.

Concentration also alters the distribution of variance across time.

In diversified income architectures with low correlation, variance events tend to be staggered. A decline in one stream may not coincide with decline in another. The system experiences partial contraction rather than total contraction. Margin absorbs some impact. Liquidity absorbs residual timing mismatch. Recovery in one stream may offset weakness in another before structural strain accumulates.

In concentrated architectures, variance events cluster by definition. When the dominant inflow driver weakens, the majority of dependable capacity weakens simultaneously. The system experiences synchronous contraction.

Synchronous contraction is structurally more dangerous than staggered contraction because it compresses margin across all inflows at once. Liquidity tiers must respond immediately. There is no internal offset mechanism.

Revenue stream correlation therefore functions as a variance synchronizer.

Correlation can be explicit or implicit. Explicit correlation exists when multiple compensation elements are tied to identical metrics, such as base salary, bonus, and equity derived from the same employer's performance. Implicit correlation exists when streams are tied to similar macro drivers, such as regional economic cycles or industry demand patterns.

Implicit correlation is often underestimated because inflows appear separate on the surface. A consulting contract and a speaking engagement may appear distinct. If both are tied to the same industry's expansion phase, contraction will likely affect both simultaneously.

Fragility amplification occurs when correlated streams support fixed-cost structures calibrated to peak conditions.

Consider a professional whose reliable floor is derived from salary and expected bonus within a single firm. Rigid commitments are calibrated to that composite income. During expansion, bonus is consistent and equity appreciates. During contraction, bonus declines and equity value falls. If salary is also at risk, total dependable capacity may drop significantly within one cycle.

Even if margin was proportionate under peak conditions, contraction magnitude may exceed margin quickly because correlation concentrates impact.

Exposure stacking intensifies this effect.

Stacking occurs when multiple financial dimensions depend on the same driver. Income, equity compensation, retirement investments, and even real estate value may all be tied to one sector. Under expansion, stacking produces rapid wealth accumulation. Under contraction, stacking produces simultaneous stress across income, asset value, and potentially liquidity if assets are illiquid.

Stacking reduces independence among system components.

Independence is central to resilience. When system components fail independently, overall system remains stable. When components fail simultaneously, stress multiplies.

Professional identity lock-in contributes to stacking by reducing mobility between drivers.

When skills are narrowly specialized and networks concentrated within a single ecosystem, income adaptability declines. Even if opportunities exist outside that ecosystem, transition costs may be high. Dependable capacity becomes path-dependent on continuation of specific sector health.

Income rigidity in this context is not contractual but structural. It arises from limited alternative inflow options.

Structural decoupling strategies do not require equal diversification across numerous streams. Excessive fragmentation increases coordination cost and reduces efficiency. Decoupling requires partial independence.

For example, a professional employed in one industry may develop advisory relationships in adjacent but less correlated sectors. Alternatively, income derived from intellectual property, education, or services with broader demand base may introduce partial independence from employer performance.

Partial independence reduces synchrony of contraction.

The objective is not to eliminate concentration but to reduce the probability that total dependable capacity declines sharply within a single variance event.

Proportional exposure means that the degree of concentration should be consistent with the system's structural buffers.

If income concentration is extreme, structural buffers—margin and liquidity—must be correspondingly robust. If buffers are limited, concentration should be moderated through layering.

This alignment is mechanical.

A highly concentrated income base with narrow margin and shallow liquidity is structurally fragile. A highly concentrated income base with wide margin and deep runway can be stable despite exposure.

Conversely, moderate diversification does not compensate for excessive rigidity density and insufficient liquidity.

Income fragility under macro reversion demonstrates these interactions.

Macro reversion refers to normalization of economic conditions after expansion. During expansion, concentration may appear low risk because volatility is suppressed and demand strong. Under reversion, demand weakens across correlated sectors. Bonuses decline. equity compensation underperforms. Contract opportunities shrink.

If rigid commitments were scaled during expansion and liquidity buffers not widened proportionally, contraction collides with concentrated exposure. Liquidity tiers activate immediately. Runway shortens rapidly.

In diversified architectures with partially independent inflows, macro reversion may reduce one stream significantly while leaving others relatively intact. Margin absorbs greater share of contraction. Liquidity use is moderated. Runway remains intact.

Configuration redesign under concentrated exposure requires analysis of driver independence.

The first step is mapping income streams to underlying drivers. If multiple streams share primary driver, correlation is high. If drivers differ materially, correlation is lower.

The second step is measuring rigidity density relative to concentrated dependable capacity. If rigid load consumes high percentage of dependable income derived from one driver, fragility is elevated.

The third step is evaluating liquidity runway under scenario where dominant driver contracts materially. If runway is insufficient to sustain obligations across defined contraction horizon, either buffers must deepen or concentration must decrease.

Redesign may involve reducing rigidity density, widening margin, deepening liquidity, or introducing partially independent inflow sources.

The structural objective remains proportional exposure.

Concentration can increase income magnitude and efficiency. Diversification can reduce income growth rate or increase administrative complexity. The appropriate balance depends on volatility characteristics of primary driver and structural tolerance capacity.

Over long horizons, systems that ignore exposure concentration often experience episodic stress tied to sector cycles. Systems that calibrate exposure relative to buffers experience moderated cycles.

When dependable capacity is tightly coupled to one driver, fragility increases. When dependable capacity is distributed across partially independent drivers, fragility decreases.

Architecture determines whether variance in one domain propagates to entire system or remains localized.

Exposure concentration must therefore be treated as core structural variable alongside margin and liquidity.

Stability requires that exposure amplification be matched with structural buffers sufficient to absorb synchronized contraction.

When exposure is calibrated proportionally to tolerance, the system can sustain concentration without brittleness.

When exposure exceeds tolerance capacity, fragility is embedded even during prosperity.

Configuration, not income magnitude, determines whether concentration becomes growth engine or instability multiplier.

Exposure concentration also affects how quickly dependable capacity can be restored after contraction.

In a concentrated income structure, restoration depends on recovery of the dominant driver. If that driver experiences prolonged weakness, income recovery may be delayed. Even if alternative opportunities exist, transition into them may require retraining, network expansion, or reputational repositioning. Recovery velocity is constrained by dependency on one ecosystem.

In a partially decoupled structure, restoration can occur through multiple pathways. If one driver weakens, other drivers may remain intact or recover more quickly. The system has parallel recovery channels. Dependable capacity can stabilize before full macro normalization occurs.

Recovery velocity is a structural function of exposure dispersion.

When rigidity density is high and exposure concentration is high, recovery becomes doubly constrained. Obligations require immediate income restoration, yet restoration pathways are narrow. Liquidity runway determines how long the system can wait for primary driver recovery. If runway is insufficient, forced structural contraction may occur before recovery materializes.

This is the mechanism by which concentration converts macro variance into personal instability.

Correlation between income and asset value further complicates recovery.

If income and invested assets are tied to the same sector, contraction reduces both cash inflow and balance sheet strength simultaneously. Liquidity derived from asset liquidation may be impaired if asset values are depressed during contraction. Strategic reserves invested heavily in correlated assets may decline at the same time income declines.

Stacked exposure thus compresses both income and liquidity simultaneously.

Even if nominal liquidity appears adequate under stable conditions, effective liquidity during sector contraction may be reduced. Asset values decline, limiting available reserves. Strategic runway shortens in practice.

This is fragility amplification.

Professional identity lock-in reinforces delayed recovery.

If career progression has been optimized around a single employer or sector, skill sets may not translate immediately into adjacent markets.

Income substitution requires time. During that time, liquidity must sustain obligations. If liquidity is insufficient relative to rigidity density, structural pressure increases rapidly.

Therefore, exposure concentration must be evaluated not only by probability of contraction but by expected recovery time under contraction.

Drivers with high volatility and long recovery horizons require wider margin and deeper liquidity to maintain tolerance. Drivers with moderate volatility and short recovery horizons may require less buffer.

Configuration redesign under concentrated exposure is iterative.

Reducing concentration does not require immediate equal distribution across multiple sources. It requires introducing partial independence incrementally.

For example, income layering through advisory engagements in adjacent sectors, product development serving broader markets, or remote opportunities decoupled from local industry cycles can reduce synchronization risk. Even modest uncorrelated inflow can reduce total contraction magnitude during sector downturn.

However, layering must be evaluated relative to complexity cost. Excessive fragmentation may reduce efficiency, dilute focus, and impair primary income growth. Structural decoupling aims for independence of drivers, not maximal number of streams.

Proportional exposure remains the guiding principle.

If dominant inflow represents eighty percent of dependable capacity, and that inflow is volatile and correlated with invested assets, structural buffers must be substantial. If dominant inflow represents fifty percent and secondary inflow is independent, buffer requirements may be lower for equivalent tolerance.

The relationship between exposure concentration and buffer depth is nonlinear. Small reductions in correlation can significantly reduce synchronized contraction risk.

Income fragility under macro reversion is often misinterpreted as unpredictable misfortune. Structurally, it is predictable when concentration, correlation, and insufficient buffers coincide.

During expansion, concentrated exposure produces rapid income growth. Rigidity may scale. Liquidity may be deployed into correlated assets. Margin may not widen proportionally. Under reversion, contraction impacts income, asset values, and liquidity simultaneously. Structural buffers activate quickly.

In diversified architectures, contraction may reduce primary income while secondary streams remain stable or decline less severely. Asset diversification may preserve liquidity value. Margin absorbs part of contraction. Runway remains intact.

The contrast is mechanical.

Exposure concentration is neither inherently prudent nor inherently reckless. It is a leverage on variance magnitude.

High concentration increases expected variance magnitude relative to dependable capacity. Low concentration reduces magnitude but may reduce efficiency and peak income growth.

The structural decision is not whether to concentrate but whether concentration is matched by adequate tolerance.

Income fragility emerges when concentration exceeds tolerance capacity.

Configuration redesign can also occur through adjustment of rigidity density rather than solely through income layering.

If concentrated exposure is unavoidable due to professional specialization, rigid commitments must remain conservative relative to reliable floor. Margin must be wide. Liquidity runway must be deep. Contract stack duration must align with expected recovery horizons.

This preserves tolerance despite concentration.

Conversely, if rigid commitments are high and liquidity shallow, concentration must be reduced to maintain stability.

Structural alignment is the objective.

Over long horizons, industries cycle. Firms rise and decline. Compensation structures evolve. Professionals who treat exposure concentration as static risk are surprised by variance. Professionals who treat it as design variable calibrate buffers and layering accordingly.

Exposure concentration interacts with every prior mechanism: margin calibration, liquidity design, rigidity density, and structural drift.

When concentration, high rigidity, and thin liquidity coexist, fragility is embedded even in prosperity. When concentration is balanced with proportional buffers and independent layering, stability persists despite volatility.

Income fragility is the sensitivity of dependable capacity to single-driver variance.

Stability requires that no single driver possess disproportionate power to compress the entire system beyond its tolerance capacity.

Configuration determines whether concentration functions as efficiency amplifier or as instability multiplier.

Commitment Stacking and Obligation Fragility

An obligation is a structural load imposed on dependable capacity. It is not merely an expense; it is a claim on future inflow that persists across time. When modeled mechanically, each obligation functions as a load vector directed against the reliable income floor. The magnitude of the vector is the payment amount. The direction is temporal—recurring across defined intervals. The persistence of the vector is determined by duration and enforceability.

Load vectors differ in rigidity.

Fixed commitments are vectors with predetermined magnitude, timing, and duration. Their enforceability is external. Deviation produces contractual consequence. The system cannot adjust these vectors without renegotiation or breach. Their structural behavior is predictable but inflexible.

Semi-fixed commitments are vectors with recurring magnitude and timing but limited adjustability. Their enforceability is softer but not negligible. Cancellation or modification often requires notice, coordination, or cost. Under stable conditions, semi-fixed vectors appear flexible. Under variance, their persistence approximates fixed load because friction inhibits immediate removal.

Behavioral commitments are internally enforced load vectors. They are not contractually binding but become persistent through habit or expectation. Their magnitude may fluctuate, but their recurrence creates quasi-rigidity. When behavioral commitments are treated as baseline rather than discretionary, they exert structural pressure comparable to semi-fixed load.

Together, these vectors form the obligation profile.

An isolated load vector can be evaluated against dependable capacity with relative clarity. When multiple vectors are layered sequentially across time, stacking occurs.

Stacking is the accumulation of load vectors without proportional recalibration of structural distance. Each new commitment is superimposed upon existing vectors. The system does not replace one load with another; it layers additional magnitude and duration onto the structure.

Stacking is not inherently destabilizing. It becomes destabilizing when cumulative load approaches or exceeds the tolerance defined by margin and liquidity architecture.

Over time, stacking changes system behavior.

Each additional load vector reduces discretionary capacity and narrows magnitude tolerance. More importantly, it reduces structural elasticity. Elasticity is the ability to absorb variation without modifying commitments. As load vectors accumulate, elasticity declines even if total income rises.

Stacking transforms obligations from discrete decisions into an integrated load-bearing framework.

Because commitments are rarely added simultaneously, stacking proceeds incrementally. A housing commitment is followed by transportation financing. Education financing overlaps with service contracts. Insurance layers accumulate. Subscription structures embed recurring semi-fixed load. Each layer is rational in isolation. Collectively, they create a composite load profile.

This composite profile becomes structural anchor.

Anchors resist movement. When income varies, the anchored system must adjust around fixed points. The more anchors present, the fewer degrees of freedom remain for adjustment.

Anchoring also alters the system's center of gravity. As rigid load density increases, a larger share of dependable capacity is pre-committed before discretionary allocation occurs. Variance then interacts with a smaller residual domain. Even moderate income contraction can eliminate residual capacity entirely, forcing engagement with rigid commitments.

Obligation stacking therefore alters variance transmission pathways.

In low-density systems, variance is absorbed within discretionary space. In stacked systems, variance reaches rigid load more quickly because discretionary buffer is thin.

Duration amplifies stacking.

When load vectors persist for extended horizons, stacking effects compound. A short-duration obligation may expire before new layers accumulate significantly. A long-duration obligation persists while new layers are added on top. Overlapping durations create multi-layered load stacks that extend across macro cycles.

As stacking progresses, the system becomes increasingly path-dependent. Decisions made in earlier periods constrain options in later periods because load vectors remain active. Recalibration opportunities narrow.

Stacking also increases structural inertia.

Inertia is resistance to reconfiguration. A system with minimal load vectors can adjust commitments rapidly under variance. A system with numerous long-duration vectors must navigate contractual constraints, negotiation friction, and timing restrictions to reduce load.

The interaction between stacking and exposure concentration is direct.

If dependable capacity is concentrated in a single inflow source, and obligations are heavily stacked, the system is doubly exposed. Income contraction impacts a high-density load structure simultaneously. Margin may be bypassed quickly. Liquidity tiers may activate rapidly.

Even with disciplined margin and liquidity design, excessive stacking relative to dependable capacity creates nonlinear fragility.

Nonlinearity emerges because load vectors do not scale proportionally with income contraction. A ten percent income reduction in a lightly stacked system reduces surplus. In a heavily stacked system, the same reduction may eliminate surplus entirely and begin to threaten rigid commitments.

This threshold effect is structural.

Below a certain stacking density, variance remains contained. Beyond that density, small additional load layers produce disproportionate fragility. The relationship between stacking and tolerance is not linear; it accelerates as density increases.

Behavioral commitments contribute to this acceleration when treated as fixed baseline. If internal expectations solidify into persistent load vectors, structural density increases without formal contracts. Under variance, these behavioral loads may resist adjustment nearly as strongly as fixed obligations because lifestyle reconfiguration carries friction.

Commitment stacking is therefore not limited to legally binding contracts. It includes all recurring claims treated as non-negotiable within the system.

The cumulative effect of stacking is a reduction in structural degrees of freedom.

Degrees of freedom define how many variables can adjust under variance without altering core commitments. As load vectors accumulate in magnitude and duration, degrees of freedom decline. The system becomes constrained.

Constraint is not immediately visible under stable inflow. It reveals itself when inflow deviates.

Obligation fragility emerges when stacked load vectors exceed the structural capacity defined by dependable income, calibrated margin, and available liquidity runway. The fragility is embedded in configuration long before visible instability appears.

Stacking is gradual. Fragility is threshold-based.

When stacking remains proportionate to dependable capacity and supported by adequate buffers, the system remains tolerant. When stacking advances beyond proportional alignment, the system crosses into brittle territory even if income remains high.

Obligations are not neutral. They are structural forces acting continuously against dependable capacity. When layered without proportional recalibration, they transform architecture from elastic to rigid.

The mechanism of fragility begins with stacking.

Obligation fragility intensifies when stacked load vectors are not only numerous but synchronized.

Synchronization risk arises when multiple commitments share similar payment timing within the income cycle. Even if aggregate rigidity density is proportionate to dependable capacity, temporal clustering can produce localized compression.

Each load vector has a magnitude and a timing coordinate. When timing coordinates align closely, the system experiences concentrated outflow demand within narrow windows. If inflow timing is not equally concentrated or does not precede outflow clustering, sequencing pressure emerges.

In a distributed timing profile, obligations are staggered across the cycle. Outflow is smoothed. Operational liquidity absorbs minor timing differences without activating higher-tier reserves. In a synchronized profile, several rigid and semi-fixed commitments draw against capacity simultaneously. Even with adequate annual margin, short-term stress can arise.

Synchronization converts magnitude sufficiency into timing fragility.

Consider a system where rigid commitments consume sixty percent of reliable monthly income. If these commitments are distributed evenly across the month and inflow is also evenly distributed, operational liquidity remains stable. If instead the majority of rigid commitments are due within the first five days of the cycle while inflow arrives later, operational liquidity must bridge the entire clustered load.

If operational liquidity is thin, the system escalates to tactical reserves unnecessarily. Tactical liquidity intended for moderate income deviation becomes an operational timing buffer. Tier separation collapses.

Repeated synchronization stress erodes tactical reserves even in the absence of true income contraction.

Synchronization also interacts with stacking density.

In low-density systems, even clustered payments may be manageable because discretionary capacity remains large relative to total load. In high-density systems, clustered payments leave minimal residual capacity. The same timing pattern produces greater strain.

Clustering therefore multiplies the effect of stacking.

Sequencing risk increases as synchronization increases.

Sequencing risk is not solely a function of income volatility. It is a function of relative timing between inflow and stacked obligations. When multiple obligations align temporally, the system becomes sensitive to minor inflow delays. A delayed payment or timing mismatch can trigger cascading adjustments because several commitments are waiting simultaneously.

In distributed timing configurations, a delay may affect only one or two commitments before inflow stabilizes. In synchronized configurations, a delay can affect many commitments at once.

The result is nonlinear activation of reserves.

Operational liquidity is designed to absorb routine timing mismatches. When synchronization is high, operational liquidity requirements increase substantially. If operational liquidity is not scaled proportionally to clustered load, tactical reserves become the first line of defense.

Tactical reserve activation in response to sequencing rather than true income contraction reduces runway unnecessarily. Over time, this increases fragility even if dependable capacity remains stable.

Synchronization also amplifies cognitive load.

When numerous commitments converge within short windows, monitoring intensity increases. Payment timing must be managed precisely. Minor administrative errors become consequential. The system requires precision to avoid unnecessary reserve activation.

Precision can compensate temporarily for synchronization. It does not eliminate structural vulnerability.

As stacking density rises, synchronization effects compound.

New commitments are often layered without regard to existing timing structure. Renewal cycles, loan origination dates, subscription start dates, and contractual billing cycles accumulate organically. Without structural review, clustering emerges unintentionally.

Clustering is therefore often an artifact of incremental stacking rather than deliberate design.

Under stable inflow, clustering may not produce visible strain. Under moderate variance or minor inflow delays, synchronization becomes a multiplier.

Synchronization interacts with exposure concentration as well.

If income inflow itself is concentrated—such as a single monthly payment or irregular bonus structure—while obligations are clustered before or around inflow receipt, sequencing fragility increases sharply. In such systems, operational liquidity must be deep relative to clustered load to prevent escalation.

If income is diversified across multiple inflow dates and obligations are distributed, sequencing risk declines.

Temporal alignment between inflow and outflow is therefore a structural variable.

Obligation synchronization does not change total load magnitude. It changes stress distribution across time.

In systems with adequate margin and deep liquidity tiers, synchronization may be tolerable because buffers absorb clustering without degradation. In compressed systems, synchronization accelerates reserve drawdown and exposes fragility quickly.

The structural objective is not perfect staggering of obligations but proportional alignment between clustered load and operational liquidity capacity.

If clustered obligations exceed operational liquidity consistently, the system is structurally misaligned even if aggregate annual income supports commitments.

Synchronization is often invisible in static analysis because annual totals appear manageable. Only cycle-level modeling reveals timing concentration.

When stacked obligations align temporally and interact with high rigidity density, the system becomes sensitive to small disturbances that would otherwise be contained.

Obligation fragility therefore has two axes: magnitude stacking and temporal synchronization.

Magnitude stacking narrows structural distance. Temporal synchronization concentrates stress within cycles. When both are present, tolerance declines nonlinearly.

Stacked and synchronized commitments transform ordinary timing variability into structural stress events.

The mechanism of fragility intensifies when load vectors not only accumulate but converge.

Proceeding further requires modeling how duration stacking extends these effects across macro horizons.

Duration stacking introduces a second dimension of obligation fragility: temporal rigidity across macro horizons.

Each commitment possesses a duration parameter. Short-duration commitments provide periodic recalibration points. Long-duration commitments lock load vectors into the structure for extended periods. When multiple long-duration commitments overlap, duration stacking occurs.

Duration stacking reduces structural flexibility because recalibration opportunities are deferred. If a single long-term obligation exists, recalibration may occur upon maturity. When multiple long-term obligations are layered sequentially, maturities extend far into the future, reducing frequency of structural reset points.

Overlapping durations create a commitment horizon that spans multiple economic cycles.

Macro cycles are characterized by expansion and contraction phases. Income volatility patterns change across these phases. When obligations extend beyond a single phase, they embed assumptions about future dependable capacity across uncertain conditions.

In lightly stacked duration profiles, a downturn may coincide with expiration of certain commitments, allowing load reduction without negotiation. In heavily stacked duration profiles, downturns occur while commitments remain locked.

Duration stacking therefore converts cyclical variance into prolonged structural exposure.

The interaction between duration stacking and liquidity runway is direct.

Liquidity provides time-based tolerance. Duration stacking extends exposure time. If commitments extend for decades while liquidity runway covers only months, the system must rely on continued dependable capacity for the majority of the obligation horizon.

If income volatility widens during that horizon and liquidity cannot sustain prolonged contraction, structural pressure intensifies.

Duration stacking also interacts with exposure concentration.

If income is concentrated in a single sector and long-duration commitments extend across that sector's potential cyclical downturn, fragility increases. The system is exposed both to income contraction and to rigid load persistence simultaneously.

If income is partially decoupled across sectors with different cycle timing, duration stacking may be less dangerous because contraction in one sector may not coincide with peak rigidity stress.

The structural risk emerges when long-duration commitments align with concentrated and correlated income streams.

Duration stacking also influences recovery velocity.

In a system with short-duration commitments, recovery from contraction may be assisted by natural expiration of obligations. As commitments mature, load declines without active restructuring. In a system with long-duration stacking, recovery requires either income restoration or active renegotiation because commitments remain constant.

Renegotiation introduces friction. It may involve penalties, refinancing costs, or contractual constraints. Therefore, duration stacking increases the cost of structural adjustment under variance.

The longer the overlapping durations, the greater the structural inertia.

Inertia reduces the system's ability to adapt to changing income structures. If a professional's reliable floor shifts downward permanently due to industry disruption, long-duration stacking prevents rapid alignment between load and new dependable capacity.

Liquidity runway may sustain obligations temporarily, but if duration exposure extends beyond runway, reserves deplete before structural realignment can occur.

Duration stacking also compounds with synchronization.

When multiple long-duration commitments share similar origination dates, their maturity timelines may align. This creates concentrated recalibration windows but also concentrated stress windows if refinancing or renewal occurs under unfavorable conditions.

If interest rate environments shift or macro conditions deteriorate during maturity clustering, renegotiation may be expensive.

Thus duration stacking can create both rigidity during term and vulnerability at maturity.

Another dimension emerges in relation to margin compression.

As commitments are layered across long horizons, margin may appear adequate in early years of stacking. Over time, as additional layers accumulate, margin narrows gradually while duration exposure extends further. The system becomes tightly coupled to income continuity across decades.

The fragility is not visible until income variance intersects with stacked duration at scale.

Duration stacking also affects professional optionality.

Long-term obligations constrain geographic mobility, career shifts, and risk-taking. If dependable capacity is partially dependent on concentration within a single industry and long-duration commitments limit relocation or transition flexibility, exposure becomes structurally embedded.

Optionality is reduced not because of behavioral hesitation but because structural commitments limit degrees of freedom.

The relationship between duration stacking and macro reversion is particularly significant.

In expansion phases, long-duration commitments may appear safe because income is stable and growth strong. Under reversion, if contraction persists longer than liquidity runway, duration stacking forces difficult choices. Either commitments must be renegotiated under unfavorable conditions, or reserves must be exhausted.

If duration exposure had been shorter or staggered, natural expiration might reduce load during contraction without forced action.

Therefore, duration stacking increases dependency on macro continuity.

The structural objective is not avoidance of long-duration commitments. Many necessary obligations inherently span long horizons. The objective is proportional alignment between duration exposure, income volatility characteristics, and liquidity runway.

If income is volatile or concentrated, duration stacking must be accompanied by wider margin and deeper liquidity. If liquidity runway is shallow and income concentration high, long-duration stacking increases fragility sharply.

Duration stacking converts temporal uncertainty into fixed structural exposure.

When layered with magnitude stacking and synchronization, it produces multidimensional fragility: magnitude rigidity, timing concentration, and horizon lock-in.

These dimensions interact nonlinearly.

A lightly stacked system may absorb duration exposure because magnitude density is low. A heavily stacked system with synchronized timing and concentrated income cannot absorb long-duration rigidity without significant buffer depth.

Commitment fragility therefore increases as duration stacking extends beyond the tolerance capacity defined by margin, liquidity, and exposure dispersion.

Obligations are not merely present-cycle constraints. They are future-cycle claims that persist regardless of macro state.

When multiple future-cycle claims overlap across extended horizons, the system becomes sensitive to deviations not only today but across years.

Duration stacking embeds variance risk into the long-term structure.

The next mechanism emerges when compression intersects with stacked obligations and minor income contraction activates nonlinear stress thresholds.

When margin is wide and obligations are lightly stacked, income contraction interacts first with surplus. The system absorbs moderate deviation within discretionary space. Stacked commitments remain insulated because structural distance exists.

Under compression, stacked commitments alter this sequence.

When rigidity density is high and duration stacking extensive, even minor income contraction can bypass residual surplus rapidly. The residual domain is thin. A small reduction in dependable capacity may eliminate surplus entirely and begin to press against rigid load within one or two cycles.

This is margin bypass.

Margin bypass occurs when the reduction in income magnitude exceeds available discretionary buffer immediately, forcing engagement with rigid commitments or liquidity tiers without intermediate absorption.

In lightly stacked systems, margin bypass requires significant contraction. In heavily stacked systems, margin bypass can be triggered by moderate contraction because the buffer zone between dependable capacity and load is narrow.

Once bypass occurs, liquidity activation follows.

Operational liquidity addresses sequencing friction. Tactical liquidity addresses moderate contraction. Under heavy stacking, tactical reserves may be activated not because contraction is extreme but because stacked obligations reduce discretionary absorption capacity.

If tactical reserves are drawn repeatedly to sustain baseline, runway shortens quickly. If strategic reserves are then activated to cover extended contraction, tier collapse begins.

Tier collapse is the merging of operational, tactical, and strategic liquidity functions due to persistent stress.

When operational liquidity is insufficient to manage synchronized obligations, tactical reserves are used operationally. When tactical reserves are insufficient to cover prolonged contraction, strategic reserves are used tactically. The distinct purposes of each tier blur.

As tiers collapse, runway compresses nonlinearly.

Nonlinearity arises because reserve drawdown under stacked commitments accelerates once thresholds are crossed. For example, if rigid load consumes eighty percent of dependable capacity and income contracts by fifteen percent, surplus may disappear entirely and a portion of rigid commitments may require liquidity support. Each cycle then requires reserve deployment equal to the deficit.

If contraction persists for several cycles, reserves decline linearly while stress increases geometrically because declining reserves reduce future tolerance.

The threshold between stability and fragility is not smooth. It is abrupt once stacking density exceeds certain proportions relative to dependable capacity.

Below threshold, variance is contained within surplus and modest liquidity use. Above threshold, variance cascades through liquidity tiers rapidly and forces structural decisions.

Escalation triggers are therefore configuration-dependent.

A ten percent contraction in dependable capacity may be inconsequential in a system where rigid commitments consume fifty percent of income and liquidity runway is deep. The same contraction may be destabilizing in a system where rigid commitments consume eighty-five percent of income and runway is shallow.

Stacked commitments amplify contraction magnitude by increasing the proportion of income pre-committed.

Synchronization further accelerates escalation. If multiple rigid commitments are due during contraction cycles, liquidity drawdown occurs in concentrated bursts. Tactical reserves may deplete in one clustered window rather than gradually.

Duration stacking prevents natural relief. Obligations persist across cycles, so contraction stress is cumulative rather than episodic.

Exposure concentration compounds escalation.

If income contraction is driven by weakness in a single concentrated driver and obligations are heavily stacked, contraction magnitude may exceed margin quickly. Liquidity tiers activate in full rather than partially.

Nonlinear fragility thresholds can be conceptualized as density breakpoints.

At low rigidity density, the system absorbs moderate contraction with minimal reserve use. At moderate density, contraction activates tactical reserves but recovery is feasible. At high density, contraction activates strategic reserves immediately and may exhaust them within short duration.

These breakpoints are not visible during stable inflow because commitments are met without strain. They become visible only when dependable capacity deviates.

Behavioral commitments can also function as escalation multipliers.

If behavioral load vectors are treated as non-negotiable baseline, discretionary contraction may be delayed even when income declines. This accelerates liquidity drawdown because adjustment to flexible categories is postponed.

The structural issue is not behavior but classification. When internally defined commitments are treated as fixed, stacking density increases effectively.

Escalation under compression often appears sudden because threshold effects are crossed quickly.

A system may operate near capacity for extended periods without visible stress. When income contracts modestly, escalation appears disproportionate. In reality, fragility was embedded in stacking density and duration layering.

Once liquidity tiers collapse and reserves decline below critical runway levels, structural decisions become unavoidable.

Structural decisions at that stage are constrained by duration stacking and exposure concentration. Renegotiation may be costly. Income substitution may be slow. Options narrow.

Obligation fragility therefore operates through amplification pathways.

Magnitude stacking reduces buffer width. Synchronization concentrates stress temporally. Duration stacking locks load across cycles. Exposure concentration amplifies contraction magnitude. Liquidity tier collapse accelerates reserve depletion.

Together, these mechanisms produce nonlinear outcomes.

Stability under variance requires that stacked commitments remain proportionate to dependable capacity and supported by liquidity runway sufficient to absorb moderate contraction without triggering tier collapse.

When stacking exceeds proportional alignment, fragility remains latent until triggered by variance.

The system does not degrade linearly with stacking. It crosses thresholds.

Understanding these thresholds is essential for calibrating obligation profile relative to dependable floor.

The final structural consideration concerns how commitment profiles can be recalibrated to reduce fragility without eliminating necessary obligations.

Obligation fragility can be reduced only through structural recalibration of load vectors. Recalibration does not eliminate commitments; it modifies their density, duration, synchronization, or proportional alignment with dependable capacity.

Load density can be adjusted by reducing the aggregate magnitude of fixed and semi-fixed vectors relative to reliable income floor. When aggregate load declines as a percentage of dependable capacity, margin buffer widens automatically. Variance must be larger before margin bypass occurs. Escalation thresholds shift outward.

Duration exposure can be adjusted by limiting overlap of long-term commitments. When long-duration vectors are staggered rather than layered simultaneously, recalibration windows increase in frequency. Expiration of one commitment creates structural breathing space before new long-duration vectors are added. This reduces horizon lock-in and improves adaptability across macro cycles.

Synchronization can be reduced by distributing timing coordinates of load vectors across the income cycle. When clustered commitments are separated temporally, operational liquidity demands decline. Tactical reserves are preserved for genuine contraction rather than sequencing friction. Tier separation remains intact.

These adjustments alter fragility not through advice but through mechanical redistribution of structural stress, and recalibration must remain proportional to dependable floor and volatility characteristics.

If income volatility band is wide or exposure concentration high, obligation density must remain conservative relative to reliable capacity. If income is narrow-band and diversified, slightly higher density may be sustainable without breaching tolerance thresholds. Proportionality is central.

Load calibration also interacts with liquidity runway.

If duration stacking is unavoidable due to necessary long-term commitments, liquidity runway must extend sufficiently to bridge expected contraction horizons. If runway cannot be extended, duration exposure must remain limited. Alignment between horizon of obligations and runway depth prevents tier collapse under moderate variance.

Structural decoupling of obligations from single inflow drivers also reduces fragility.

When commitments are structured such that their sustainability does not depend exclusively on one concentrated income source, exposure risk declines. This does not require fragmentation of commitments but requires that their aggregate magnitude remains supportable under stress scenarios defined by concentrated inflow contraction.

Recalibration mechanisms therefore operate along four axes: magnitude density, temporal distribution, duration layering, and alignment with volatility characteristics.

Reducing magnitude density increases margin buffer. Reducing synchronization decreases sequencing stress. Limiting overlapping durations increases recalibration frequency. Aligning commitment profile with volatility band ensures that stress scenarios do not exceed structural tolerance prematurely.

Fragility declines when these axes are proportionate to dependable capacity.

Obligation profile must be evaluated dynamically.

As income grows, stacking pressure increases because additional dependable capacity tempts expansion of commitments. If new load vectors are layered without proportional widening of structural distance, fragility accumulates gradually. Maintenance discipline requires that load growth lag buffer growth.

If exposure concentration increases due to career shifts or industry changes, commitment density must adjust downward or liquidity runway must expand upward to maintain tolerance.

Structural decoupling is not a single event. It is an ongoing calibration process responding to shifts in dependable capacity and macro conditions.

Obligation fragility emerges when commitment profile outpaces the structural buffers designed to support it. Recalibration restores proportional alignment.

When magnitude density is moderated, synchronization distributed, duration staggered, and exposure aligned with volatility characteristics, nonlinear fragility thresholds shift outward. Minor variance remains contained within surplus and operational liquidity. Moderate contraction activates tactical reserves without collapsing tiers. Prolonged contraction can be sustained within strategic runway without forced structural breach.

Commitments are not inherently destabilizing. They become destabilizing when stacked beyond proportional tolerance.

A durable financial architecture maintains structural distance not only on the income side but on the commitment side. Load vectors must remain calibrated to dependable capacity and supported by time-based buffers.

When obligation stacking is controlled and aligned with structural tolerance, the system retains elasticity under variance. When stacking proceeds unchecked relative to margin, liquidity, and exposure profile, fragility becomes embedded even during stable conditions.

Commitment profile is therefore a primary determinant of stability.

Asset Structure and Liquidity Mismatch Risk

An obligation is a structural load imposed on dependable capacity. It is not merely an expense; it is a claim on future inflow that persists across time. When modeled mechanically, each obligation functions as a load vector directed against the reliable income floor. The magnitude of the vector is the payment amount. The direction is temporal—recurring across defined intervals. The persistence of the vector is determined by duration and enforceability.

Load vectors differ in rigidity.

Fixed commitments are vectors with predetermined magnitude, timing, and duration. Their enforceability is external. Deviation produces contractual consequence. The system cannot adjust these vectors without renegotiation or breach. Their structural behavior is predictable but inflexible.

Semi-fixed commitments are vectors with recurring magnitude and timing but limited adjustability. Their enforceability is softer but not negligible. Cancellation or modification often requires notice, coordination, or cost. Under stable conditions, semi-fixed vectors appear flexible. Under variance, their persistence approximates fixed load because friction inhibits immediate removal.

Behavioral commitments are internally enforced load vectors. They are not contractually binding but become persistent through habit or expectation. Their magnitude may fluctuate, but their recurrence creates quasi-rigidity. When behavioral commitments are treated as baseline rather than discretionary, they exert structural pressure comparable to semi-fixed load.

Together, these vectors form the obligation profile.

An isolated load vector can be evaluated against dependable capacity with relative clarity. When multiple vectors are layered sequentially across time, stacking occurs.

Stacking is the accumulation of load vectors without proportional recalibration of structural distance. Each new commitment is superimposed upon existing vectors. The system does not replace one load with another; it layers additional magnitude and duration onto the structure.

Stacking is not inherently destabilizing. It becomes destabilizing when cumulative load approaches or exceeds the tolerance defined by margin and liquidity architecture.

Over time, stacking changes system behavior.

Each additional load vector reduces discretionary capacity and narrows magnitude tolerance. More importantly, it reduces structural elasticity. Elasticity is the ability to absorb variation without modifying commitments. As load vectors accumulate, elasticity declines even if total income rises.

Stacking transforms obligations from discrete decisions into an integrated load-bearing framework.

Because commitments are rarely added simultaneously, stacking proceeds incrementally. A housing commitment is followed by transportation financing. Education financing overlaps with service contracts. Insurance layers accumulate. Subscription structures embed recurring semi-fixed load. Each layer is rational in isolation. Collectively, they create a composite load profile.

This composite profile becomes structural anchor.

Anchors resist movement. When income varies, the anchored system must adjust around fixed points. The more anchors present, the fewer degrees of freedom remain for adjustment.

Anchoring also alters the system's center of gravity. As rigid load density increases, a larger share of dependable capacity is pre-committed before discretionary allocation occurs. Variance then interacts with a smaller residual domain. Even moderate income contraction can eliminate residual capacity entirely, forcing engagement with rigid commitments.

Obligation stacking therefore alters variance transmission pathways.

In low-density systems, variance is absorbed within discretionary space. In stacked systems, variance reaches rigid load more quickly because discretionary buffer is thin.

Duration amplifies stacking.

When load vectors persist for extended horizons, stacking effects compound. A short-duration obligation may expire before new layers accumulate significantly. A long-duration obligation persists while new layers are added on top. Overlapping durations create multi-layered load stacks that extend across macro cycles.

As stacking progresses, the system becomes increasingly path-dependent. Decisions made in earlier periods constrain options in later periods because load vectors remain active. Recalibration opportunities narrow.

Stacking also increases structural inertia.

Inertia is resistance to reconfiguration. A system with minimal load vectors can adjust commitments rapidly under variance. A system with numerous long-duration vectors must navigate contractual constraints, negotiation friction, and timing restrictions to reduce load.

The interaction between stacking and exposure concentration is direct.

If dependable capacity is concentrated in a single inflow source, and obligations are heavily stacked, the system is doubly exposed. Income contraction impacts a high-density load structure simultaneously. Margin may be bypassed quickly. Liquidity tiers may activate rapidly.

Even with disciplined margin and liquidity design, excessive stacking relative to dependable capacity creates nonlinear fragility.

Nonlinearity emerges because load vectors do not scale proportionally with income contraction. A ten percent income reduction in a lightly stacked system reduces surplus. In a heavily stacked system, the same reduction may eliminate surplus entirely and begin to threaten rigid commitments.

This threshold effect is structural.

Below a certain stacking density, variance remains contained. Beyond that density, small additional load layers produce disproportionate fragility. The relationship between stacking and tolerance is not linear; it accelerates as density increases.

Behavioral commitments contribute to this acceleration when treated as fixed baseline. If internal expectations solidify into persistent load vectors, structural density increases without formal contracts. Under variance, these behavioral loads may resist adjustment nearly as strongly as fixed obligations because lifestyle reconfiguration carries friction.

Commitment stacking is therefore not limited to legally binding contracts. It includes all recurring claims treated as non-negotiable within the system.

The cumulative effect of stacking is a reduction in structural degrees of freedom.

Degrees of freedom define how many variables can adjust under variance without altering core commitments. As load vectors accumulate in magnitude and duration, degrees of freedom decline. The system becomes constrained.

Constraint is not immediately visible under stable inflow. It reveals itself when inflow deviates.

Obligation fragility emerges when stacked load vectors exceed the structural capacity defined by dependable income, calibrated margin, and available liquidity runway. The fragility is embedded in configuration long before visible instability appears.

Stacking is gradual. Fragility is threshold-based.

When stacking remains proportionate to dependable capacity and supported by adequate buffers, the system remains tolerant. When stacking advances beyond proportional alignment, the system crosses into brittle territory even if income remains high.

Obligations are not neutral. They are structural forces acting continuously against dependable capacity. When layered without proportional recalibration, they transform architecture from elastic to rigid.

The mechanism of fragility begins with stacking.

Obligation fragility intensifies when stacked load vectors are not only numerous but synchronized.

Synchronization risk arises when multiple commitments share similar payment timing within the income cycle. Even if aggregate rigidity density is proportionate to dependable capacity, temporal clustering can produce localized compression.

Each load vector has a magnitude and a timing coordinate. When timing coordinates align closely, the system experiences concentrated outflow demand within narrow windows. If inflow timing is not equally concentrated or does not precede outflow clustering, sequencing pressure emerges.

In a distributed timing profile, obligations are staggered across the cycle. Outflow is smoothed. Operational liquidity absorbs minor timing differences without activating higher-tier reserves. In a synchronized profile, several rigid and semi-fixed commitments draw against capacity simultaneously. Even with adequate annual margin, short-term stress can arise.

Synchronization converts magnitude sufficiency into timing fragility.

Consider a system where rigid commitments consume sixty percent of reliable monthly income. If these commitments are distributed evenly across the month and inflow is also evenly distributed, operational liquidity remains stable. If instead the majority of rigid commitments are due within the first five days of the cycle while inflow arrives later, operational liquidity must bridge the entire clustered load.

If operational liquidity is thin, the system escalates to tactical reserves unnecessarily. Tactical liquidity intended for moderate income deviation becomes an operational timing buffer. Tier separation collapses.

Repeated synchronization stress erodes tactical reserves even in the absence of true income contraction.

Synchronization also interacts with stacking density.

In low-density systems, even clustered payments may be manageable because discretionary capacity remains large relative to total load. In high-density systems, clustered payments leave minimal residual capacity. The same timing pattern produces greater strain.

Clustering therefore multiplies the effect of stacking.

Sequencing risk increases as synchronization increases.

Sequencing risk is not solely a function of income volatility. It is a function of relative timing between inflow and stacked obligations. When multiple obligations align temporally, the system becomes sensitive to minor inflow delays. A delayed payment or timing mismatch can trigger cascading adjustments because several commitments are waiting simultaneously.

In distributed timing configurations, a delay may affect only one or two commitments before inflow stabilizes. In synchronized configurations, a delay can affect many commitments at once.

The result is nonlinear activation of reserves.

Operational liquidity is designed to absorb routine timing mismatches. When synchronization is high, operational liquidity requirements increase substantially. If operational liquidity is not scaled proportionally to clustered load, tactical reserves become the first line of defense.

Tactical reserve activation in response to sequencing rather than true income contraction reduces runway unnecessarily. Over time, this increases fragility even if dependable capacity remains stable.

Synchronization also amplifies cognitive load.

When numerous commitments converge within short windows, monitoring intensity increases. Payment timing must be managed precisely. Minor administrative errors become consequential. The system requires precision to avoid unnecessary reserve activation.

Precision can compensate temporarily for synchronization. It does not eliminate structural vulnerability.

As stacking density rises, synchronization effects compound.

New commitments are often layered without regard to existing timing structure. Renewal cycles, loan origination dates, subscription start dates, and contractual billing cycles accumulate organically. Without structural review, clustering emerges unintentionally.

Clustering is therefore often an artifact of incremental stacking rather than deliberate design.

Under stable inflow, clustering may not produce visible strain. Under moderate variance or minor inflow delays, synchronization becomes a multiplier.

Synchronization interacts with exposure concentration as well.

If income inflow itself is concentrated—such as a single monthly payment or irregular bonus structure—while obligations are clustered before or around inflow receipt, sequencing fragility increases sharply. In such systems, operational liquidity must be deep relative to clustered load to prevent escalation.

If income is diversified across multiple inflow dates and obligations are distributed, sequencing risk declines.

Temporal alignment between inflow and outflow is therefore a structural variable.

Obligation synchronization does not change total load magnitude. It changes stress distribution across time.

In systems with adequate margin and deep liquidity tiers, synchronization may be tolerable because buffers absorb clustering without degradation. In compressed systems, synchronization accelerates reserve drawdown and exposes fragility quickly.

The structural objective is not perfect staggering of obligations but proportional alignment between clustered load and operational liquidity capacity.

If clustered obligations exceed operational liquidity consistently, the system is structurally misaligned even if aggregate annual income supports commitments.

Synchronization is often invisible in static analysis because annual totals appear manageable. Only cycle-level modeling reveals timing concentration.

When stacked obligations align temporally and interact with high rigidity density, the system becomes sensitive to small disturbances that would otherwise be contained.

Obligation fragility therefore has two axes: magnitude stacking and temporal synchronization.

Magnitude stacking narrows structural distance. Temporal synchronization concentrates stress within cycles. When both are present, tolerance declines nonlinearly.

Stacked and synchronized commitments transform ordinary timing variability into structural stress events.

The mechanism of fragility intensifies when load vectors not only accumulate but converge.

Proceeding further requires modeling how duration stacking extends these effects across macro horizons.

Duration stacking introduces a second dimension of obligation fragility: temporal rigidity across macro horizons.

Each commitment possesses a duration parameter. Short-duration commitments provide periodic recalibration points. Long-duration commitments lock load vectors into the structure for extended periods. When multiple long-duration commitments overlap, duration stacking occurs.

Duration stacking reduces structural flexibility because recalibration opportunities are deferred. If a single long-term obligation exists, recalibration may occur upon maturity. When multiple long-term obligations are layered sequentially, maturities extend far into the future, reducing frequency of structural reset points.

Overlapping durations create a commitment horizon that spans multiple economic cycles.

Macro cycles are characterized by expansion and contraction phases. Income volatility patterns change across these phases. When obligations extend beyond a single phase, they embed assumptions about future dependable capacity across uncertain conditions.

In lightly stacked duration profiles, a downturn may coincide with expiration of certain commitments, allowing load reduction without negotiation. In heavily stacked duration profiles, downturns occur while commitments remain locked.

Duration stacking therefore converts cyclical variance into prolonged structural exposure.

The interaction between duration stacking and liquidity runway is direct.

Liquidity provides time-based tolerance. Duration stacking extends exposure time. If commitments extend for decades while liquidity runway covers only months, the system must rely on continued dependable capacity for the majority of the obligation horizon.

If income volatility widens during that horizon and liquidity cannot sustain prolonged contraction, structural pressure intensifies.

Duration stacking also interacts with exposure concentration.

If income is concentrated in a single sector and long-duration commitments extend across that sector's potential cyclical downturn, fragility increases. The system is exposed both to income contraction and to rigid load persistence simultaneously.

If income is partially decoupled across sectors with different cycle timing, duration stacking may be less dangerous because contraction in one sector may not coincide with peak rigidity stress.

The structural risk emerges when long-duration commitments align with concentrated and correlated income streams.

Duration stacking also influences recovery velocity.

In a system with short-duration commitments, recovery from contraction may be assisted by natural expiration of obligations. As commitments mature, load declines without active restructuring. In a system with long-duration stacking, recovery requires either income restoration or active renegotiation because commitments remain constant.

Renegotiation introduces friction. It may involve penalties, refinancing costs, or contractual constraints. Therefore, duration stacking increases the cost of structural adjustment under variance.

The longer the overlapping durations, the greater the structural inertia.

Inertia reduces the system's ability to adapt to changing income structures. If a professional's reliable floor shifts downward permanently due to industry disruption, long-duration stacking prevents rapid alignment between load and new dependable capacity.

Liquidity runway may sustain obligations temporarily, but if duration exposure extends beyond runway, reserves deplete before structural realignment can occur.

Duration stacking also compounds with synchronization.

When multiple long-duration commitments share similar origination dates, their maturity timelines may align. This creates concentrated recalibration windows but also concentrated stress windows if refinancing or renewal occurs under unfavorable conditions.

If interest rate environments shift or macro conditions deteriorate during maturity clustering, renegotiation may be expensive.

Thus duration stacking can create both rigidity during term and vulnerability at maturity.

Another dimension emerges in relation to margin compression.

As commitments are layered across long horizons, margin may appear adequate in early years of stacking. Over time, as additional layers accumulate, margin narrows gradually while duration exposure extends further. The system becomes tightly coupled to income continuity across decades.

The fragility is not visible until income variance intersects with stacked duration at scale.

Duration stacking also affects professional optionality.

Long-term obligations constrain geographic mobility, career shifts, and risk-taking. If dependable capacity is partially dependent on concentration within a single industry and long-duration commitments limit relocation or transition flexibility, exposure becomes structurally embedded.

Optionality is reduced not because of behavioral hesitation but because structural commitments limit degrees of freedom.

The relationship between duration stacking and macro reversion is particularly significant.

In expansion phases, long-duration commitments may appear safe because income is stable and growth strong. Under reversion, if contraction persists longer than liquidity runway, duration stacking forces difficult choices. Either commitments must be renegotiated under unfavorable conditions, or reserves must be exhausted.

If duration exposure had been shorter or staggered, natural expiration might reduce load during contraction without forced action.

Therefore, duration stacking increases dependency on macro continuity.

The structural objective is not avoidance of long-duration commitments. Many necessary obligations inherently span long horizons. The objective is proportional alignment between duration exposure, income volatility characteristics, and liquidity runway.

If income is volatile or concentrated, duration stacking must be accompanied by wider margin and deeper liquidity. If liquidity runway is shallow and income concentration high, long-duration stacking increases fragility sharply.

Duration stacking converts temporal uncertainty into fixed structural exposure.

When layered with magnitude stacking and synchronization, it produces multidimensional fragility: magnitude rigidity, timing concentration, and horizon lock-in.

These dimensions interact nonlinearly.

A lightly stacked system may absorb duration exposure because magnitude density is low. A heavily stacked system with synchronized timing and concentrated income cannot absorb long-duration rigidity without significant buffer depth.

Commitment fragility therefore increases as duration stacking extends beyond the tolerance capacity defined by margin, liquidity, and exposure dispersion.

Obligations are not merely present-cycle constraints. They are future-cycle claims that persist regardless of macro state.

When multiple future-cycle claims overlap across extended horizons, the system becomes sensitive to deviations not only today but across years.

Duration stacking embeds variance risk into the long-term structure.

The next mechanism emerges when compression intersects with stacked obligations and minor income contraction activates nonlinear stress thresholds.

When margin is wide and obligations are lightly stacked, income contraction interacts first with surplus. The system absorbs moderate deviation within discretionary space. Stacked commitments remain insulated because structural distance exists.

Under compression, stacked commitments alter this sequence.

When rigidity density is high and duration stacking extensive, even minor income contraction can bypass residual surplus rapidly. The residual domain is thin. A small reduction in dependable capacity may eliminate surplus entirely and begin to press against rigid load within one or two cycles.

This is margin bypass.

Margin bypass occurs when the reduction in income magnitude exceeds available discretionary buffer immediately, forcing engagement with rigid commitments or liquidity tiers without intermediate absorption.

In lightly stacked systems, margin bypass requires significant contraction. In heavily stacked systems, margin bypass can be triggered by moderate contraction because the buffer zone between dependable capacity and load is narrow.

Once bypass occurs, liquidity activation follows.

Operational liquidity addresses sequencing friction. Tactical liquidity addresses moderate contraction. Under heavy stacking, tactical reserves may be activated not because contraction is extreme but because stacked obligations reduce discretionary absorption capacity.

If tactical reserves are drawn repeatedly to sustain baseline, runway shortens quickly. If strategic reserves are then activated to cover extended contraction, tier collapse begins.

Tier collapse is the merging of operational, tactical, and strategic liquidity functions due to persistent stress.

When operational liquidity is insufficient to manage synchronized obligations, tactical reserves are used operationally. When tactical reserves are insufficient to cover prolonged contraction, strategic reserves are used tactically. The distinct purposes of each tier blur.

As tiers collapse, runway compresses nonlinearly.

Nonlinearity arises because reserve drawdown under stacked commitments accelerates once thresholds are crossed. For example, if rigid load consumes eighty percent of dependable capacity and income contracts by fifteen percent, surplus may disappear entirely and a portion of rigid commitments may require liquidity support. Each cycle then requires reserve deployment equal to the deficit.

If contraction persists for several cycles, reserves decline linearly while stress increases geometrically because declining reserves reduce future tolerance.

The threshold between stability and fragility is not smooth. It is abrupt once stacking density exceeds certain proportions relative to dependable capacity.

Below threshold, variance is contained within surplus and modest liquidity use. Above threshold, variance cascades through liquidity tiers rapidly and forces structural decisions.

Escalation triggers are therefore configuration-dependent.

A ten percent contraction in dependable capacity may be inconsequential in a system where rigid commitments consume fifty percent of income and liquidity runway is deep. The same contraction may be destabilizing in a system where rigid commitments consume eighty-five percent of income and runway is shallow.

Stacked commitments amplify contraction magnitude by increasing the proportion of income pre-committed.

Synchronization further accelerates escalation. If multiple rigid commitments are due during contraction cycles, liquidity drawdown occurs in concentrated bursts. Tactical reserves may deplete in one clustered window rather than gradually.

Duration stacking prevents natural relief. Obligations persist across cycles, so contraction stress is cumulative rather than episodic.

Exposure concentration compounds escalation.

If income contraction is driven by weakness in a single concentrated driver and obligations are heavily stacked, contraction magnitude may exceed margin quickly. Liquidity tiers activate in full rather than partially.

Nonlinear fragility thresholds can be conceptualized as density breakpoints.

At low rigidity density, the system absorbs moderate contraction with minimal reserve use. At moderate density, contraction activates tactical reserves but recovery is feasible. At high density, contraction activates strategic reserves immediately and may exhaust them within short duration.

These breakpoints are not visible during stable inflow because commitments are met without strain. They become visible only when dependable capacity deviates.

Behavioral commitments can also function as escalation multipliers.

If behavioral load vectors are treated as non-negotiable baseline, discretionary contraction may be delayed even when income declines. This accelerates liquidity drawdown because adjustment to flexible categories is postponed.

The structural issue is not behavior but classification. When internally defined commitments are treated as fixed, stacking density increases effectively.

Escalation under compression often appears sudden because threshold effects are crossed quickly.

A system may operate near capacity for extended periods without visible stress. When income contracts modestly, escalation appears disproportionate. In reality, fragility was embedded in stacking density and duration layering.

Once liquidity tiers collapse and reserves decline below critical runway levels, structural decisions become unavoidable.

Structural decisions at that stage are constrained by duration stacking and exposure concentration. Renegotiation may be costly. Income substitution may be slow. Options narrow.

Obligation fragility therefore operates through amplification pathways.

Magnitude stacking reduces buffer width. Synchronization concentrates stress temporally. Duration stacking locks load across cycles. Exposure concentration amplifies contraction magnitude. Liquidity tier collapse accelerates reserve depletion.

Together, these mechanisms produce nonlinear outcomes.

Stability under variance requires that stacked commitments remain proportionate to dependable capacity and supported by liquidity runway sufficient to absorb moderate contraction without triggering tier collapse.

When stacking exceeds proportional alignment, fragility remains latent until triggered by variance.

The system does not degrade linearly with stacking. It crosses thresholds.

Understanding these thresholds is essential for calibrating obligation profile relative to dependable floor.

The final structural consideration concerns how commitment profiles can be recalibrated to reduce fragility without eliminating necessary obligations.

Obligation fragility can be reduced only through structural recalibration of load vectors. Recalibration does not eliminate commitments; it modifies their density, duration, synchronization, or proportional alignment with dependable capacity.

Load density can be adjusted by reducing the aggregate magnitude of fixed and semi-fixed vectors relative to reliable income floor. When aggregate load declines as a percentage of dependable capacity, margin buffer widens automatically. Variance must be larger before margin bypass occurs. Escalation thresholds shift outward.

Duration exposure can be adjusted by limiting overlap of long-term commitments. When long-duration vectors are staggered rather than layered simultaneously, recalibration windows increase in frequency. Expiration of one commitment creates structural breathing space before new long-duration vectors are added. This reduces horizon lock-in and improves adaptability across macro cycles.

Synchronization can be reduced by distributing timing coordinates of load vectors across the income cycle. When clustered commitments are separated temporally, operational liquidity demands decline. Tactical reserves are preserved for genuine contraction rather than sequencing friction. Tier separation remains intact.

These adjustments alter fragility not through advice but through mechanical redistribution of structural stress.

Recalibration must remain proportional to dependable floor and volatility characteristics.

If income volatility band is wide or exposure concentration high, obligation density must remain conservative relative to reliable capacity. If income is narrow-band and diversified, slightly higher density may be sustainable without breaching tolerance thresholds. Proportionality is central.

Load calibration also interacts with liquidity runway.

If duration stacking is unavoidable due to necessary long-term commitments, liquidity runway must extend sufficiently to bridge expected contraction horizons. If runway cannot be extended, duration exposure must remain limited. Alignment between horizon of obligations and runway depth prevents tier collapse under moderate variance.

Structural decoupling of obligations from single inflow drivers also reduces fragility.

When commitments are structured such that their sustainability does not depend exclusively on one concentrated income source, exposure risk declines. This does not require fragmentation of commitments but requires that their aggregate magnitude remains supportable under stress scenarios defined by concentrated inflow contraction.

Recalibration mechanisms therefore operate along four axes: magnitude density, temporal distribution, duration layering, and alignment with volatility characteristics.

Reducing magnitude density increases margin buffer. Reducing synchronization decreases sequencing stress. Limiting overlapping durations increases recalibration frequency. Aligning commitment profile with volatility band ensures that stress scenarios do not exceed structural tolerance prematurely.

Fragility declines when these axes are proportionate to dependable capacity, and obligation profile must be evaluated dynamically.

As income grows, stacking pressure increases because additional dependable capacity tempts expansion of commitments. If new load vectors are layered without proportional widening of structural distance, fragility accumulates gradually. Maintenance discipline requires that load growth lag buffer growth.

If exposure concentration increases due to career shifts or industry changes, commitment density must adjust downward or liquidity runway must expand upward to maintain tolerance.

Structural decoupling is not a single event. It is an ongoing calibration process responding to shifts in dependable capacity and macro conditions.

Obligation fragility emerges when commitment profile outpaces the structural buffers designed to support it. Recalibration restores proportional alignment.

When magnitude density is moderated, synchronization distributed, duration staggered, and exposure aligned with volatility characteristics, nonlinear fragility thresholds shift outward. Minor variance remains contained within surplus and operational liquidity. Moderate contraction activates tactical reserves without collapsing tiers. Prolonged contraction can be sustained within strategic runway without forced structural breach.

Commitments are not inherently destabilizing. They become destabilizing when stacked beyond proportional tolerance. A durable financial architecture maintains structural distance not only on the income side but on the commitment side. Load vectors must remain calibrated to dependable capacity and supported by time-based buffers.

When obligation stacking is controlled and aligned with structural tolerance, the system retains elasticity under variance. When stacking proceeds unchecked relative to margin, liquidity, and exposure profile, fragility becomes embedded even during stable conditions.

Commitment profile is therefore a primary determinant of stability.

Variance Propagation and Stress Transmission Dynamics

Variance is a disturbance entering the financial architecture from outside or emerging within it. It may take the form of income contraction, expense shock, asset revaluation, timing disruption, or correlated macro contraction. Structurally, variance is not defined by its magnitude alone but by how it propagates through the system once introduced.

A disturbance first contacts a boundary condition. If it is income-based, it alters dependable capacity. If obligation-based, it increases load magnitude. If liquidity-based, it reduces available time buffer. If asset-based, it alters conversion capacity or balance sheet resilience. Each entry point determines initial propagation vector.

Transmission pathways are defined by coupling between system components.

Income contraction reduces margin first. If margin absorbs the deviation, propagation halts locally. If contraction exceeds surplus, liquidity tiers activate. If liquidity activation persists, asset conversion may follow. If asset conversion is constrained or correlated with income decline, structural pressure intensifies.

Obligation shock increases load density. Increased load reduces available margin instantly. If margin becomes negative relative to dependable capacity, liquidity tiers engage. If liquidity is insufficient, obligations may require renegotiation or liquidation of assets. Transmission moves from load to liquidity to assets.

Asset revaluation alters perceived buffer strength. If asset values decline but liquidity tiers remain intact and obligations proportionate, propagation may remain localized to balance sheet metrics. If asset values decline in conjunction with income contraction, effective buffer shrinks at the same time load remains constant, accelerating transmission.

Liquidity disturbance—such as depletion of reserves due to prior variance—reduces time tolerance. When new variance enters, absence of liquidity increases propagation speed because the buffer absorption sequence shortens.

Coupling density determines translation speed.

Coupling density is the degree to which system components are interdependent. High rigidity density couples income tightly to obligations. High exposure concentration couples income to asset values. High illiquidity couples asset value to delayed conversion. High synchronization couples obligations to timing stress.

When coupling density is low, disturbances remain localized. Income contraction affects surplus but not obligations. Asset volatility affects net worth but not liquidity. Obligation increase affects margin but not runway significantly. Each domain absorbs variance within its buffer zone.

When coupling density is high, disturbances translate rapidly across domains. Income contraction reduces margin, activates liquidity, forces asset conversion, and may interact with correlated asset decline simultaneously. Propagation is immediate and multidirectional.

Localized propagation occurs when buffers are sufficient and coupling moderate. A moderate income dip reduces surplus for one or two cycles. Liquidity remains intact. Assets unaffected. Obligations stable. System remains coherent.

System-wide propagation occurs when disturbance bypasses containment thresholds and activates multiple domains sequentially.

Containment thresholds are defined by buffer capacities and proportional alignment.

Margin provides first containment threshold. If disturbance magnitude is less than structural distance between dependable capacity and load, absorption is localized. Liquidity provides second containment threshold. If disturbance persists beyond margin absorption, reserves extend tolerance in time. Asset convertibility provides third containment threshold. If liquidity depletes, assets may provide extension.

If all thresholds are aligned proportionately, propagation decelerates at each stage.

If thresholds are narrow due to compression, propagation accelerates.

Transmission acceleration under compression occurs because surplus is thin and liquidity shallow. A moderate disturbance immediately exceeds margin. Liquidity tiers activate quickly. If reserves are limited, asset conversion is required sooner. If assets are illiquid or correlated, realized losses amplify stress.

Compression reduces the distance between containment thresholds, shortening the absorption sequence.

Feedback loops emerge when disturbance alters structural parameters.

Income contraction may lead to reduced discretionary spending, but if obligations are rigid, adjustment options are limited. Liquidity drawdown reduces future runway, increasing sensitivity to subsequent disturbances. Asset liquidation under stress may reduce balance sheet strength, increasing exposure to future variance.

These feedback loops increase system rigidity relative to reduced capacity.

For example, if income contraction persists and liquidity is used to sustain commitments, the system becomes increasingly dependent on income recovery because reserves decline. Declining reserves increase fragility, which may restrict professional mobility or strategic shifts that could improve income prospects. Rigidity thus feeds back into income fragility.

Variance clustering intensifies transmission.

Disturbances rarely occur in isolation. Income contraction may coincide with asset volatility. Expense shocks may coincide with timing disruptions. When disturbances cluster temporally, buffer absorption is tested simultaneously across domains.

Temporal compression occurs when multiple variance events arrive within a short window. Even if each event individually is within tolerance, combined effect may exceed containment thresholds.

For example, a moderate income dip combined with unexpected expense and asset decline may collectively exceed margin and deplete liquidity tiers rapidly.

Nonlinear escalation dynamics arise because buffer capacities are finite and sequential.

When first threshold is breached, pressure shifts to second. When second is breached, pressure shifts to third. Each shift reduces optionality and increases urgency. Urgency may force suboptimal decisions, such as forced asset liquidation under adverse conditions, which further reduces resilience.

The escalation is nonlinear because once certain thresholds are crossed, incremental additional disturbance produces disproportionate impact.

Structural containment depends on decoupling and buffer depth.

If income, obligations, liquidity, and assets are proportionately aligned and partially independent, disturbances slow as they move through the system. If these domains are tightly coupled and compressed, disturbances cascade rapidly.

Cascade failure occurs when propagation cannot be contained at any threshold and multiple domains degrade simultaneously.

In cascade failure, income contraction activates liquidity depletion. Liquidity depletion forces asset liquidation. Asset liquidation under correlation reduces balance sheet strength and may impair future income prospects. Obligations remain rigid, increasing load density relative to reduced capacity. Each domain reinforces contraction in the others.

Structural containment prevents cascade by ensuring that disturbance energy dissipates at each boundary.

When margin is sufficient, disturbance energy dissipates in surplus. When liquidity runway is deep, disturbance energy dissipates in time extension. When assets are liquid and diversified, disturbance energy dissipates in conversion without excessive loss. When obligations are proportionate and not excessively stacked or synchronized, load remains manageable.

Propagation dynamics become clearer when modeled across multiple disturbance cycles rather than a single shock event.

A single moderate contraction tests containment thresholds once. A multi-cycle disturbance tests decay rate of buffers and recovery velocity between shocks.

Consider a system with moderate coupling density and proportionate buffers. A fifteen percent income contraction enters in cycle one. Margin absorbs part of the contraction. Liquidity covers the residual. Assets remain untouched. Income partially recovers in cycle two. Liquidity stabilizes. Propagation halts.

Now consider repeated contraction before recovery completes. A second disturbance arrives while liquidity tiers are partially depleted. The same magnitude shock now produces greater structural impact because containment capacity has declined. Buffer depth is path-dependent.

Propagation speed is not constant. It increases when buffers thin.

In lightly coupled systems, repeated shocks may remain localized because domains are partially independent. Income contraction may not coincide with asset decline. Obligations remain proportionate. Liquidity rebuilds between cycles. Propagation remains segmented.

In tightly coupled systems, repeated shocks compound. Income contraction reduces margin. Liquidity depletes. Asset values decline due to correlation. Asset conversion under stress reduces balance sheet strength.

Subsequent contraction meets weaker buffers. Each cycle shortens the containment sequence.

This is cumulative propagation.

Cumulative propagation differs from cascade failure. Cascade failure is immediate system-wide breakdown. Cumulative propagation is gradual degradation of containment thresholds across cycles until a threshold is crossed.

Recovery velocity becomes central to durability.

If recovery velocity exceeds disturbance frequency, buffers rebuild faster than they decay. Propagation slows. If disturbance frequency exceeds recovery velocity, buffer erosion outpaces rebuilding. Containment thresholds compress over time even if individual shocks are moderate.

Recovery velocity is determined by income restoration rate, discretionary elasticity, liquidity replenishment speed, and absence of correlated asset decline.

High rigidity density reduces recovery velocity because obligations prevent rapid surplus rebuilding. High exposure concentration reduces recovery velocity because income restoration depends on single-driver recovery. High illiquidity reduces recovery velocity because assets cannot be mobilized to restore buffers quickly.

When recovery velocity declines below disturbance frequency, nonlinear escalation becomes probable even without a single catastrophic shock.

Propagation also varies by disturbance origin.

Income-origin disturbances primarily attack margin first. Asset-origin disturbances primarily attack perceived resilience but may remain localized unless liquidity or obligations are already compressed. Obligation-origin disturbances immediately alter load density and may bypass margin if introduced during compressed states.

When disturbances originate in multiple domains simultaneously—income contraction combined with asset volatility and timing disruption—containment thresholds are tested in parallel rather than sequentially. Parallel testing accelerates translation speed because multiple domains degrade at once.

Parallel degradation reduces optionality faster than sequential degradation.

Sequential propagation allows decision space between thresholds. Parallel propagation compresses decision space.

Temporal compression therefore magnifies propagation.

If disturbances are spaced widely enough for buffer rebuilding, the architecture demonstrates resilience. If disturbances cluster within short intervals, even moderate systems may experience rapid escalation because rebuilding windows vanish.

Variance propagation is not only about shock size. It is about shock sequencing relative to buffer restoration capacity.

Another propagation distinction exists between reversible and irreversible degradation.

Liquidity depletion is reversible if income recovers and reserves are rebuilt. Asset liquidation under stress may be partially irreversible if realized losses reduce future earning potential or capital growth base. Obligation renegotiation under distress may alter long-term structural terms permanently.

Propagation becomes structurally damaging when irreversible adjustments occur before containment stabilizes.

Irreversibility increases long-term fragility because future disturbances encounter reduced structural distance even if current crisis resolves.

Thus durability depends on keeping disturbances within reversible containment domains.

Architectures with sufficient margin, deep liquidity tiers, moderate coupling density, and asset convertibility aligned with obligation horizons tend to localize repeated disturbances and preserve reversibility.

Architectures with compression across these domains experience accelerated propagation, threshold crossing, and higher probability of irreversible structural degradation.

Variance transmission is therefore dynamic, time-dependent, and threshold-sensitive.

The question is not whether disturbance enters the system. It is whether the architecture slows translation sufficiently to prevent cumulative degradation across cycles.

Variance propagation is therefore a function of coupling density, buffer depth, and proportional alignment.

The system is stable not because disturbances do not occur, but because disturbances are absorbed without translating across domains in accelerating sequence.

Financial durability is defined by the ability to slow and localize variance propagation before it becomes system-wide.

The architecture either dampens disturbances or amplifies them.

Structural Thresholds and Nonlinear Breakpoints

A financial system does not deteriorate gradually in proportion to stress. It operates within tolerance bands defined by configuration-dependent thresholds. Within those bands, disturbances are absorbed with limited structural change. Once specific breakpoints are crossed, system behavior changes discontinuously.

A threshold is not an external event. It is an internal configuration boundary. It marks the point at which absorption capacity is exhausted and propagation dynamics alter.

In stable states, margin absorbs moderate magnitude variance. Liquidity absorbs duration variance. Obligations remain insulated. Asset convertibility is not required. Disturbances dissipate within surplus and time buffers. The system returns to baseline without structural modification.

Stress within this zone produces linear response. A ten percent income contraction reduces surplus proportionately. A temporary expense spike reduces available liquidity but remains within runway tolerance. Asset volatility alters net worth but not cash-flow survivability.

Linear response persists only while thresholds remain unbreached.

The first instability threshold is margin bypass.

Margin bypass occurs when disturbance magnitude exceeds the structural distance between dependable capacity and rigid load. Surplus collapses. Adjustment must move from discretionary domain into liquidity tiers. This transition marks a change in system behavior. Variance is no longer contained in magnitude; it becomes a time problem.

In lightly compressed systems, margin bypass requires significant contraction. In compressed systems, modest deviation can trigger it.

Margin bypass does not produce immediate failure. It initiates second-order dynamics. Liquidity reserves begin to compensate for lost surplus. Recovery depends on duration and depth of contraction relative to runway.

If contraction is brief and runway adequate, the system returns to stable zone. If contraction persists or buffers are shallow, the system approaches second-order breakpoint.

The second-order breakpoint is liquidity tier collapse.

Liquidity tier collapse occurs when reserves designed for sequential absorption are forced to perform outside intended scope. Operational liquidity is insufficient to manage sequencing. Tactical reserves support baseline obligations. Strategic reserves are activated to maintain continuity.

As tiers collapse into one another, runway shortens nonlinearly. Each drawdown reduces future tolerance. The time horizon within which recovery must occur compresses.

At this stage, system response is no longer proportional to disturbance magnitude. A moderate additional contraction may exhaust remaining reserves abruptly. The absorption curve steepens.

Coupling density determines threshold sensitivity.

When income is concentrated, obligations heavily stacked, assets correlated, and liquidity shallow, thresholds lie close together. Margin bypass may occur with minor contraction. Liquidity collapse may follow shortly after.

When components are partially decoupled and buffers deep, thresholds are spaced further apart. Disturbance must be larger or more prolonged to trigger breakpoint transitions.

Compression zones are defined by diminishing absorption distance between thresholds.

As rigidity density increases or liquidity declines, the gap between stable zone and instability zone narrows. Systems may operate for extended periods within narrow tolerance without visible strain. Yet they are operating near boundary conditions.

Within compression zones, absorption distance is thin. Minor additional stress can cross thresholds rapidly.

Buffer exhaustion follows acceleration curves.

When liquidity reserves are drawn to compensate for margin bypass, depletion may appear linear initially. However, as reserves decline, behavioral and structural responses can alter inflow or obligation profile. Increased stress may reduce income further or prevent proactive recalibration. This interaction can accelerate depletion.

Acceleration occurs because shrinking buffers increase sensitivity to each incremental disturbance.

Rigidity density creates tolerance cliffs.

Tolerance cliffs are points at which small reductions in dependable capacity produce disproportionate structural impact. If rigid commitments consume a high percentage of reliable income floor, even small contraction eliminates surplus entirely and forces reserve activation.

At lower rigidity density, similar contraction reduces surplus but preserves some discretionary capacity. The system remains above cliff edge.

Tolerance cliffs are not visible under stable inflow. They become apparent only when contraction tests structural limits.

Small-shock / large-response dynamics characterize systems near cliffs.

In high-density configurations, a five percent income reduction may trigger margin bypass, liquidity activation, and psychological pressure simultaneously. In lower-density configurations, a fifteen percent reduction may remain manageable within surplus.

Nonlinearity arises because response is determined by proximity to structural thresholds, not by shock magnitude alone.

Sequencing compression can also produce abrupt escalation.

If obligations are synchronized and income timing misaligns, operational liquidity may deplete rapidly within a single cycle. Even if aggregate monthly income is sufficient, timing concentration may force tactical reserve use.

When sequencing compression coincides with margin bypass, liquidity drawdown accelerates.

Recovery inversion emerges when restoration lags degradation.

Degradation under compression can occur quickly because thresholds are close. Restoration requires surplus generation and reserve rebuilding, which take time. If income recovery is gradual, restoration may lag significantly behind initial degradation.

This inversion creates asymmetry. The system falls into compressed state quickly but exits slowly.

Across multiple cycles, cumulative erosion narrows tolerance band further.

Repeated moderate contractions, even if individually survivable, can reduce liquidity and increase rigidity ratio. Each cycle begins with lower buffer. Thresholds migrate inward. Eventually, disturbance that would previously have been contained now crosses breakpoint.

Regime shift modeling describes transition from stable to compressed to unstable states.

In stable regime, thresholds are distant. Disturbances are localized. In compressed regime, thresholds are proximate. Disturbances translate quickly across domains. In unstable regime, thresholds have been crossed; liquidity tiers collapsed; obligations must be renegotiated or assets liquidated under stress.

Regime shifts are not triggered solely by external shock magnitude. They are triggered by internal configuration crossing breakpoints.

High-income systems often misinterpret prosperity as safety.

When dependable capacity is large, margin in absolute terms may appear substantial. However, if rigidity density scales proportionately and liquidity does not widen commensurately, relative distance to thresholds may remain narrow.

Absolute surplus can coexist with threshold proximity.

Breakpoint visibility is limited to stress conditions.

Under prosperity, systems near thresholds appear stable. Margin is positive. Liquidity intact. Assets appreciated. Only when disturbance tests buffer does nonlinear response reveal proximity to breakpoints.

Structural fragility differs from temporary volatility.

Temporary volatility remains within stable zone. Fragility is proximity to nonlinear breakpoints where small additional stress produces cascading change.

Pre-threshold warning patterns include declining surplus ratio relative to dependable capacity, increasing reliance on liquidity for routine adjustments, extended recovery periods after moderate disturbance, and rising rigidity percentage without proportional buffer growth.

These patterns signal migration toward compression zone.

Slow degradation occurs when repeated moderate disturbances erode buffers gradually. Abrupt collapse occurs when a disturbance crosses tolerance cliff directly due to high coupling density and shallow buffers.

Breakpoint migration occurs across time as configuration changes.

To illustrate how nonlinear breakpoints operate across time, consider a system beginning in a stable regime with moderate rigidity density and proportionate liquidity tiers.

Reliable income floor is 100 units. Rigid load is 75 units. Structural margin distance is therefore 25 units. Liquidity tiers equal 30 units distributed across operational and tactical reserves. Asset convertibility is moderate and uncorrelated with income source.

In cycle one, income contracts by 15 percent. Dependable capacity falls to 85. Margin compresses from 25 to 10. The system remains above margin bypass threshold. No liquidity activation is required. Structural state remains within linear response zone.

In cycle two, income remains at 85. No recovery has occurred. A moderate expense shock of 5 units arrives. Effective load becomes 80 against dependable capacity of 85. Margin narrows to 5. Still positive, but structural distance to threshold has shrunk materially. Liquidity remains intact, yet the system now operates near a tolerance cliff.

In cycle three, income declines an additional 5 percent to 80. Rigid load remains 75. Margin collapses to 5 before discretionary reduction. The system crosses margin bypass threshold. Liquidity activation begins.

If 5 units per cycle are drawn from liquidity to maintain obligations, reserves decline from 30 to 25, then 20, then 15 across three cycles. Depletion appears linear in absolute terms, but structural sensitivity increases nonlinearly because each successive cycle begins with thinner buffer.

At 15 units remaining, liquidity tier collapse threshold lies closer than before. Another moderate contraction of 5 units now eliminates remaining surplus entirely and accelerates drawdown to 10 within a single cycle.

This demonstrates threshold compression. The disturbance magnitude has not increased dramatically, yet structural state has shifted from stable to compressed to near-unstable because thresholds migrated inward after initial activation.

Now consider parallel threshold testing.

During cycle four, assume asset values decline 12 percent due to correlated macro contraction. Balance sheet resilience weakens at the same time liquidity has fallen to 15. If asset convertibility requires pricing concession under stress, effective conversion value may decline to 80 percent of prior mark-to-market valuation.

If income remains at 80 and rigid load at 75, the system now operates with near-zero margin, shallow liquidity, and weakened asset buffer simultaneously. Thresholds are tested in parallel rather than sequentially.

Parallel testing accelerates regime shift because containment stages no longer provide decision space between transitions. Margin bypass and liquidity depletion coincide with asset fragility. A modest additional disturbance now produces disproportionate structural change.

This is nonlinear escalation. The system does not deteriorate proportionately to shock size; it deteriorates relative to proximity to clustered breakpoints.

Recovery inversion compounds this dynamic. If income recovery begins gradually at 3 percent per cycle, dependable capacity rises from 80 to 82.4, then 84.9. However, liquidity may already be reduced to 10. Surplus rebuilding now requires multiple cycles before thresholds widen again. The system climbed down quickly but climbs back slowly.

If another disturbance arrives during recovery phase, it encounters thinner buffers than the original stable configuration. Breakpoint migration has occurred. The structural distance between stable and unstable regimes is now narrower than at baseline.

Over multiple disturbance cycles, even moderate shocks can cumulatively migrate thresholds inward until a regime shift occurs without a single catastrophic event.

This illustrates that nonlinear breakpoints are path-dependent. They are not fixed coordinates. They move according to prior absorption history, liquidity depletion, rigidity scaling, and recovery velocity.

Durability therefore depends not only on current margin and liquidity levels but on maintaining sufficient distance between thresholds to prevent clustered activation under moderate stress.

As obligations are layered, liquidity drawn, or exposure concentration increases, thresholds move inward. As margin widens, liquidity deepens, and decoupling improves, thresholds move outward.

Designing distance from nonlinear zones requires maintaining structural space between absorption thresholds.

When margin is sufficient, liquidity tiers intact, obligations proportionate, and asset convertibility aligned, thresholds are spaced apart. Disturbances must be substantial and prolonged to trigger regime shift.

When compression narrows these distances, system becomes sensitive to modest stress.

Financial stability is therefore not defined by absence of volatility but by distance from nonlinear breakpoints embedded in configuration.

The system remains durable so long as disturbances remain within structural tolerance bands.

Recovery Dynamics and Structural Rebuilding After Compression

Recovery begins when instability has been arrested. It does not begin when income stabilizes or when immediate obligations are met. Recovery is structural reconstruction, not emotional reset. It is the deliberate widening of distances that were previously compressed and the repositioning of thresholds that had migrated inward.

Stabilization and restoration are distinct states.

Stabilization occurs when acute stress has been contained. Obligations are current. Liquidity tiers, even if diminished, are no longer in active collapse. Income contraction has ceased accelerating. The system has stopped degrading.

Restoration requires re-expansion of structural buffers to levels that reestablish tolerance bands beyond nonlinear breakpoints. Stabilization halts descent. Restoration rebuilds distance from thresholds.

In compressed systems, stabilization may occur at lower structural altitude than prior equilibrium. Liquidity tiers may be depleted. Obligations may have been renegotiated under constraint. Assets may have been liquidated at depressed valuations. Dependable capacity may have shifted.

The architecture after compression is not identical to its prior configuration.

Recovery therefore operates within altered constraints.

Buffer rebuilding velocity is typically slower than degradation velocity.

During compression, degradation can accelerate due to threshold effects. Liquidity may deplete quickly once margin bypass occurs. Asset values may decline rapidly under forced liquidation. Obligation stress may escalate abruptly.

Rebuilding buffers requires surplus generation sustained across cycles. Surplus must exceed current obligations to widen margin and replenish liquidity. If dependable capacity has contracted permanently or obligations remain elevated, surplus regeneration may be limited.

This creates recovery asymmetry.

The system may fall into compressed state in a short interval but require extended cycles to rebuild structural distance. During early recovery, surplus is thin because obligations remain and liquidity reserves are depleted. Margin may be positive but narrow. Liquidity tiers may be partially rebuilt but fragile.

Surplus regeneration under reduced structural distance is constrained by existing rigidity density.

If obligations were only partially recalibrated during compression, surplus available for rebuilding buffers is limited. Recovery must allocate surplus between liquidity replenishment, asset base reconstruction, and potential obligation reduction.

Sequencing of liquidity replenishment matters.

When tier collapse occurred during compression, operational liquidity may have been supported by tactical reserves and tactical reserves by strategic reserves. Rebuilding must reverse this cascade.

Operational liquidity must be restored first to prevent sequencing stress from prematurely activating higher tiers again. Tactical reserves must then be rebuilt to cover moderate variance. Strategic runway must be extended last to restore long-horizon tolerance.

If rebuilding skips tiers and attempts to restore long-term buffers before stabilizing operational liquidity, minor disturbances may reactivate collapse.

Asset base rebuilding after forced conversion introduces additional lag.

Assets liquidated under stress often realize losses relative to prior valuations. Rebuilding requires capital accumulation over time. If income recovery is gradual, asset reconstruction may lag liquidity replenishment.

Path dependence emerges here.

The post-compression architecture reflects the order in which buffers were depleted and obligations adjusted. If assets were sold disproportionately relative to obligations, the rebuilt balance sheet may be more liquid but less capitalized. If obligations were reduced aggressively while assets preserved, surplus regeneration may be stronger.

Recovery trajectory depends on which domains absorbed loss.

Obligation recalibration after threshold breach may alter future tolerance.

If obligations were renegotiated downward or durations shortened during compression, rigidity density may be lower in recovery phase. This can accelerate surplus regeneration. If obligations were preserved at high density and only liquidity absorbed stress, recovery may be slower because surplus must first rebuild liquidity before widening margin materially.

Recovery asymmetry also appears in income dynamics.

Recovery must also be modeled across multiple disturbance cycles rather than a single compression event. A system that has stabilized after one contraction remains structurally vulnerable if rebuilding occurs while disturbance frequency remains elevated. If a second moderate contraction arrives before liquidity tiers are fully restored, the same magnitude shock produces greater structural strain because absorption distance has not been rebuilt. Recovery under repeated disturbance therefore becomes path-sensitive.

Consider a system that has restored operational liquidity but not tactical reserves. A new income contraction bypasses margin and immediately engages partially restored liquidity. Because reserve depth is thinner than pre-compression levels, containment thresholds are reached sooner. The system may not cascade, but rebuilding velocity slows further as surplus must again be diverted toward stabilization instead of expansion. Each partial rebuilding interrupted by new variance extends recovery horizon nonlinearly.

Repeated interruption increases structural fatigue. Obligations that survived the first compression may become proportionately heavier relative to reduced surplus if rebuilding stalls. Asset reconstruction may lag further behind liquidity restoration. Recovery therefore depends not only on surplus magnitude but on disturbance spacing relative to buffer regeneration rate. If disturbance frequency exceeds regeneration velocity, the system oscillates within compression zone rather than exiting it.

This multi-cycle modeling clarifies why some systems appear to "recover" yet remain structurally fragile for extended periods. Visible stress subsides, but threshold distance remains thin because rebuilding has been repeatedly interrupted before full restoration of structural altitude.

Recovery must also be modeled across multiple disturbance cycles rather than a single compression event. A system that has stabilized after one contraction remains structurally vulnerable if rebuilding occurs while disturbance frequency remains elevated. If a second moderate contraction arrives before liquidity tiers are fully restored, the same magnitude shock produces greater structural strain because absorption distance has not been rebuilt. Recovery under repeated disturbance therefore becomes path-sensitive.

Consider a system that has restored operational liquidity but not tactical reserves. A new income contraction bypasses margin and immediately engages partially restored liquidity. Because reserve depth is thinner than pre-compression levels, containment thresholds are reached sooner. The system may not cascade, but rebuilding velocity slows further as surplus must again be diverted toward stabilization instead of expansion. Each partial rebuilding interrupted by new variance extends recovery horizon nonlinearly.

Repeated interruption increases structural fatigue. Obligations that survived the first compression may become proportionately heavier relative to reduced surplus if rebuilding stalls. Asset reconstruction may lag further behind liquidity restoration. Recovery therefore depends not only on surplus magnitude but on disturbance spacing relative to buffer regeneration rate. If disturbance frequency exceeds regeneration velocity, the system oscillates within compression zone rather than exiting it.

This multi-cycle modeling clarifies why some systems appear to "recover" yet remain structurally fragile for extended periods. Visible stress subsides, but threshold distance remains thin because rebuilding has been repeatedly interrupted before full restoration of structural altitude.

If compression was triggered by temporary contraction and income returns to prior levels quickly, surplus regeneration can be rapid provided obligations were not increased during stabilization. If contraction reflects structural shift in income capacity, recovery must occur under reduced dependable floor. Margin widening requires obligation recalibration or extended surplus retention.

Time-lag dynamics are inherent.

Buffers degrade quickly when thresholds are crossed. They rebuild slowly through accumulation. During rebuilding, the system remains closer to nonlinear zones than before compression. A moderate disturbance during early recovery can re-trigger instability if rebuilding is incomplete.

Avoiding re-compression during early recovery requires preservation of surplus as structural reinforcement rather than rapid re-expansion of commitments.

If surplus generated during early recovery is converted quickly into new obligations or illiquid assets without restoring buffer depth, thresholds may remain near. The system may appear recovered because income stabilized, but structural distance remains thin.

Structural strengthening differs from simple restoration.

Restoration seeks to return to pre-compression configuration. Strengthening seeks to migrate breakpoints outward beyond prior levels.

Strengthening involves widening margin relative to dependable capacity beyond previous density ratios, deepening liquidity runway beyond pre-crisis levels, recalibrating obligation durations to increase flexibility, and adjusting exposure concentration where contraction revealed fragility.

Breakpoint migration outward increases tolerance band and reduces sensitivity to moderate variance.

There is also a distinction between passive rebuilding and structural redesign. Passive rebuilding restores buffers in the same configuration that previously failed. Structural redesign alters configuration variables that produced compression in the first place.

If compression revealed high obligation synchronization, redesign may involve staggering commitments or reducing duration stacking rather than merely rebuilding liquidity. If compression revealed high exposure concentration, redesign may involve decoupling income drivers or diversifying asset correlation rather than simply restoring asset magnitude. If liquidity tiers collapsed sequentially without adequate separation, redesign may alter tier segmentation and trigger rules to prevent cascade replication.

Passive rebuild increases altitude without altering slope. Structural redesign changes slope itself.

When redesign is incorporated, recovery accelerates because regeneration occurs within a less compressed configuration. When redesign is ignored, recovery rebuilds previous fragility, and future disturbance may replicate prior propagation patterns with minimal variation.

Durability therefore improves only when recovery widens both buffer depth and configuration resilience simultaneously.

Designing outward breakpoint migration requires surplus allocation that prioritizes structural distance over nominal growth.

If income growth resumes, proportional scaling of obligations must lag behind buffer expansion. If asset values recover, liquidity must not be allowed to compress implicitly by converting liquid capital into illiquid holdings prematurely.

Recovery is incomplete until nonlinear thresholds are repositioned beyond stress levels previously experienced.

Over multiple cycles, recovery that strengthens architecture produces compounding resilience. Systems that merely restore prior density ratios remain susceptible to recurrence under similar variance.

Path dependence ensures that nonlinear events alter future configuration.

Forced asset liquidation may reduce exposure concentration if correlated holdings were sold. Obligation renegotiation may shorten duration stacking. Liquidity tier collapse may lead to structural redesign of buffer hierarchy. Alternatively, recovery may reconstitute previous fragility if structural recalibration is not incorporated.

Recovery dynamics therefore determine whether compression event becomes structural improvement or temporary interruption.

Stability after compression is not defined by return of income or asset values. It is defined by expansion of structural space relative to dependable capacity and obligation load.

When breakpoints migrate outward and absorption distances widen, the system exits compression regime.

When breakpoints remain proximate and surplus is thin, the system remains in latent fragility even if visible stress has receded.

Recovery is measured in structural distance regained and nonlinear zones repositioned away from operating baseline.

Structural Decoupling, Slack Economics, and Long-Horizon Optionality

Decoupling reduces the speed at which disturbance translates across financial domains. When income, obligations, liquidity, and assets are tightly linked, variance entering one domain transmits rapidly into others. When partially independent, disturbance encounters friction at each boundary. That friction is structural slack.

Translation speed is not visible in stable periods. It reveals itself only when variance appears. In a coupled architecture, income contraction alters margin immediately, activates liquidity quickly, pressures asset conversion, and interacts with obligation density within short intervals. In a decoupled architecture, contraction reduces surplus but does not immediately compromise liquidity tiers or asset integrity. The disturbance moves more slowly.

Coupled and decoupled architectures diverge most clearly over long cycles rather than single shocks.

In a baseline coupled configuration, income growth during expansion increases dependable capacity. Obligations scale proportionately or faster. Asset accumulation concentrates within correlated domains. Liquidity tiers are not widened in equal proportion because visible stress is absent. Coupling density increases as domains become more synchronized.

In a baseline decoupled configuration, income growth increases dependable capacity while obligations scale more slowly. Liquidity tiers deepen before obligations expand materially. Asset holdings are dispersed across drivers not perfectly correlated with primary income source. Slack remains visible even during prosperity.

Over a ten-year prosperity cycle, the divergence compounds.

In the coupled architecture, rising income justifies increased rigidity density. Long-duration commitments layer during stable macro conditions. Asset appreciation encourages illiquidity concentration. Liquidity, though positive in nominal terms, shrinks relative to obligation horizon. Breakpoints migrate inward relative to operating baseline.

This inward migration is subtle. Income remains strong. Asset values rise. Liquidity appears sufficient in absolute terms. Yet margin as percentage of dependable capacity may narrow. Liquidity runway measured against rigid load may shorten. Coupling between income and assets may intensify.

Prosperity miscalibration occurs when visible strength masks structural narrowing.

Scaling obligations faster than buffers during expansion reduces absorption distance without immediate consequence. Because variance is low, nonlinear thresholds remain untested. Structural slack is converted into commitment density and illiquid accumulation.

Growth-phase breakpoint migration inward is therefore common in sustained prosperity.

In the decoupled architecture, growth widens structural distance before commitments scale. Liquidity tiers deepen relative to load. Asset composition retains convertibility proportionate to volatility expectations. Obligations are staggered in duration. Exposure concentration is moderated.

Breakpoints migrate outward relative to operating baseline. Absorption zones expand.

Slack economics describes the structural underutilization of capacity as durability insurance.

Underutilization appears inefficient in static analysis. Surplus retained rather than converted into obligation or illiquid asset may reduce short-term output. However, slack reduces translation speed and increases threshold distance. It provides time and magnitude buffers that compound across cycles.

Optimization focuses on maximizing current output from dependable capacity. Decoupling focuses on preserving distance between domains.

There is a tradeoff between peak scaling and propagation speed. Systems optimized for maximum utilization exhibit faster disturbance translation. Systems designed for slower propagation sacrifice some scaling potential in exchange for resilience.

Over a fifteen-year horizon containing multiple moderate contractions, this tradeoff becomes decisive, and divergence can be modeled explicitly rather than described abstractly.

Consider two systems beginning with identical dependable capacity, identical obligation load, identical liquidity runway, and similar asset composition. In year zero, both appear stable. Margin exists. Liquidity tiers are intact. Asset convertibility is proportionate. Translation speed is moderate.

During years one through five of expansion, income increases gradually. In the coupled system, obligations scale proportionately with rising dependable capacity. Larger housing commitments, longer-duration financing, subscription layering, and illiquid asset concentration increase rigidity density. Liquidity grows nominally but declines relative to total load and obligation duration. Asset holdings increasingly correlate with primary income driver because reinvestment occurs within familiar domains. Translation speed increases incrementally though not visibly.

In the decoupled system, income growth widens surplus before obligations scale. Liquidity tiers are expanded deliberately relative to load. Asset allocation disperses across drivers not tightly synchronized with primary income source. Obligations are staggered rather than layered simultaneously. Rigidity density rises more slowly than dependable capacity. Translation speed declines slightly because slack has increased.

At year six, a moderate contraction occurs. Income declines temporarily by a fixed percentage.

In the coupled system, margin narrows sharply because rigidity density is high. Liquidity tiers activate earlier in the contraction. Asset values decline in partial synchronization due to correlated exposure. Recovery in years seven and eight restores income but liquidity rebuild lags because surplus must first service elevated obligations. Structural distance does not fully return to pre-contraction levels before expansion resumes.

In the decoupled system, margin absorbs more of the contraction because density is lower. Liquidity activation is limited to tactical reserves. Asset dispersion reduces correlated valuation decline. Recovery surplus rebuilds liquidity quickly because obligations had not scaled aggressively. Structural distance after recovery exceeds prior baseline.

Repeat this cycle at year nine and year twelve.

In the coupled system, each contraction begins from a closer proximity to nonlinear thresholds because buffer rebuilding never fully outpaced prior scaling. Liquidity runway shortens gradually. Asset convertibility declines as illiquidity accumulates. Recovery velocity slows. Optionality narrows.

In the decoupled system, each contraction begins from a wider tolerance band. Buffers absorb disturbance with minimal structural degradation. Recovery widens structural distance further. Optionality expands.

By year fifteen, the divergence is nonlinear.

The coupled system may appear successful in nominal terms — higher obligations, larger asset base, greater income scale. Yet its translation speed is high and thresholds proximate. The decoupled system may show slightly lower peak scaling but substantially greater structural distance and degrees of freedom.

Long-horizon optionality is therefore the compound result of translation speed management across cycles rather than of income magnitude alone.

In the coupled architecture, moderate contractions erode liquidity repeatedly. Because obligations are dense and assets correlated, each contraction activates reserves more aggressively. Recovery rebuilds buffers partially but obligations often remain scaled to prior peaks. Each cycle begins closer to thresholds than the previous one.

Optionality decays incrementally.

Degrees of freedom decline as liquidity rebuild lags and duration stacking persists. Even if income recovers, surplus may be directed toward restoring previous consumption or obligations rather than widening structural distance.

In the decoupled architecture, moderate contractions are absorbed primarily within surplus and tactical liquidity. Because obligation density is lower relative to dependable capacity, margin remains positive during mild downturns. Asset correlation dispersion prevents simultaneous balance sheet contraction. Recovery velocity is higher because buffers were not exhausted deeply.

Optionality compounds.

Degrees of freedom expand as surplus during recovery is retained to widen slack further. Breakpoints migrate outward after each cycle rather than inward. Over decades, the divergence between architectures widens significantly.

Long-horizon tolerance band widening versus narrowing becomes measurable.

In the coupled system, tolerance band narrows gradually. Each moderate contraction tests proximity to nonlinear zones. Buffer rebuilding struggles to exceed prior levels because obligations remain high. Asset convertibility may decline as illiquid holdings accumulate. Coupling density increases.

In the decoupled system, tolerance band widens as buffers deepen and exposure dispersion increases. Even if income volatility remains constant, structural absorption improves.

Architectural divergence after repeated moderate contractions is not linear. It accelerates.

After three or four cycles of moderate contraction across a decade, the coupled architecture may find itself operating within compression zone permanently. Surplus thin. Liquidity fragile. Thresholds proximate. A single larger disturbance may trigger nonlinear escalation quickly.

The decoupled architecture, having preserved slack and widened breakpoints outward, remains within stable regime under similar disturbances.

Controlled growth with breakpoint migration outward requires that scaling of obligations lag scaling of dependable capacity and liquidity. Asset accumulation must not eliminate convertibility needed for time-based tolerance. Exposure must remain proportionate to buffer depth.

Durable architecture is therefore a time-based decoupling discipline.

It is not defined by the absence of volatility or by consistent income growth. It is defined by persistent maintenance of translation friction between domains across cycles.

When prosperity encourages coupling, discipline preserves slack. When contraction tests thresholds, decoupling slows propagation. When recovery occurs, buffers widen further rather than merely returning to prior density.

Over ten to fifteen years, small differences in coupling discipline produce large differences in tolerance bands.

One system accumulates fragility masked by prosperity. The other accumulates optionality through preserved structural distance.

Long-horizon optionality is not an abstract concept. It is the structural ability to choose response pathways under variance without crossing nonlinear breakpoints.

Decoupling sustains that ability. Coupling erodes it gradually even while growth continues.

Durability across decades depends on how translation speed is managed during the years when stress is absent.

Governance Discipline and Anti-Drift Architecture

Financial stability does not persist automatically once structural buffers are established. It is not a static achievement secured through a single calibration of margin, liquidity, and exposure. Stability is a governed system. It requires periodic intervention to counteract drift forces that emerge during prosperity and calm cycles.

Drift is the natural recoupling of domains over time.

When income rises and volatility appears muted, surplus accumulates. Without governance discipline, surplus is converted into increased obligation density, longer duration commitments, asset concentration in appreciating sectors, and reduced liquidity relative to load. These shifts occur incrementally. Each appears rational in isolation. Collectively they narrow threshold distance.

Hidden recoupling mechanisms operate subtly.

Income growth tied to a strong sector may encourage additional investment within that same sector. Rising asset values increase perceived balance sheet strength, reducing perceived need for liquidity reserves. Stable employment history reduces perceived need for income decoupling. Obligations layered during prosperity often carry long durations, embedding optimistic assumptions about future dependable capacity.

Translation speed between domains increases gradually.

Coupling density rises because income, obligations, and assets become more synchronized around a shared macro driver. Liquidity tiers, though nominally positive, shrink relative to obligation horizon and volatility potential. Breakpoints migrate inward even as net worth increases.

Governance cadence acts as structural insulation against this drift.

Cadence refers to deliberate review intervals at which structural variables are measured relative to dependable capacity and threshold distance. Without cadence, drift accumulates unchecked across multiple cycles. With cadence, recoupling can be detected and countered before compression emerges.

Margin discipline during expansion requires that increases in dependable capacity not translate proportionately into rigid load. When income rises, margin as percentage of dependable capacity must widen before obligation scaling occurs. If margin ratio remains constant while income increases, threshold distance does not expand in relative terms.

In prosperity phases, this discipline appears conservative. However, across cycles, widened margin during expansion creates resilience during contraction.

Liquidity preservation discipline under rising income prevents silent shortening of runway.

As obligations scale and asset values appreciate, liquidity relative to rigid load must be measured. If liquidity in absolute terms grows but grows more slowly than obligation density or duration stacking, effective runway shrinks. Governance requires that liquidity tiers expand proportionally to obligation horizon and exposure characteristics.

Obligation scaling lag functions as anti-fragility mechanism.

Lag means that commitment growth trails buffer growth intentionally. When dependable capacity increases, a period of surplus retention widens structural distance before new load vectors are introduced. This increases absorption distance before coupling intensifies.

Asset concentration creep during appreciation cycles is another drift vector.

When a sector outperforms, portfolio allocation may become increasingly concentrated without new purchases. Income tied to that sector may also increase. Without rebalancing or diversification of drivers, exposure concentration rises. Balance sheet strength appears enhanced, but correlation risk increases.

Behavioral overconfidence is not treated here as psychology but as structural miscalibration.

When past volatility appears low and income growth steady, decision thresholds shift implicitly. Governance counters this by enforcing proportional alignment rules independent of recent stability. Structural calibration must be based on volatility potential, not on recent calm.

Multi-cycle modeling clarifies divergence.

Consider a ten-to-fifteen-year horizon containing expansion, contraction, partial recovery, and re-expansion.

In a governance-failure architecture, expansion phase sees rising income and asset values. Obligations scale rapidly. Liquidity grows modestly but lags obligation density. Asset concentration increases due to appreciation and reinvestment in dominant sector. Breakpoints migrate inward.

Contraction phase arrives. Income declines moderately. Margin bypass occurs earlier than in prior cycle because density is higher. Liquidity tiers activate. Asset values decline in correlated fashion. Recovery depletes reserves significantly.

Partial recovery restores income partially but not fully. Liquidity rebuilding is slow because obligations remain scaled to prior peak. Surplus is thin. Breakpoints remain proximate.

Re-expansion phase repeats scaling behavior. Obligations increase again before liquidity deepens. Asset concentration creeps further. Drift compounds across cycles.

After several such cycles, architecture operates near compression zone permanently. Even moderate disturbance may trigger nonlinear escalation.

In governance-success architecture, expansion phase sees income growth accompanied by disciplined surplus retention. Margin ratio widens. Liquidity tiers deepen relative to obligation horizon. Asset diversification counteracts concentration creep.

Contraction phase arrives. Margin absorbs moderate contraction. Liquidity tiers activate minimally. Asset volatility is partially offset by correlation dispersion. Recovery begins from higher structural altitude.

Partial recovery restores income. Surplus accelerates buffer rebuilding because obligations remained proportionate. Breakpoints migrate outward rather than inward.

Re-expansion phase begins from strengthened baseline. Obligations scale only after buffers exceed prior levels. Slack compounds.

Across multiple cycles, slack compounding produces increasing tolerance bands. Drift compounding produces narrowing tolerance bands.

Governance failure results in architectural erosion under prosperity. Governance success results in breakpoint migration outward across cycles.

Threshold monitoring metrics must focus on distance indicators rather than tactical budgeting categories.

Distance indicators include margin ratio relative to dependable capacity, liquidity runway relative to obligation horizon, exposure concentration relative to buffer depth, and asset convertibility relative to volatility band. When these distances shrink despite income growth, drift is occurring.

Structural audit framework requires periodic evaluation of coupling density.

If income and assets are increasingly correlated, if obligation density is rising faster than dependable capacity, if liquidity as proportion of rigid load is declining, thresholds are migrating inward. Audit identifies these movements before stress tests reveal them.

Optionality preservation emerges from disciplined underutilization of capacity.

When surplus is not fully converted into rigid commitments or illiquid concentration, degrees of freedom persist. During contraction, this preserved slack enables controlled adjustment rather than forced reaction.

Institutionalizing decoupling at the household level transforms governance from ad hoc response into systematic practice.

Institutionalization means that calibration of margin, liquidity, exposure, and obligation density occurs at regular intervals regardless of recent stability. It means that scaling decisions are evaluated relative to structural distance rather than solely to income magnitude.

Long-horizon durability is therefore a governance outcome rather than an income outcome.

High income without governance can produce inward breakpoint migration and eventual fragility. Moderate income with disciplined governance can produce widening tolerance bands and durable optionality across decades.

Drift is continuous. Governance must be continuous.

Over long horizons, the difference between stability and instability is rarely a single shock. It is the cumulative effect of governance discipline or its absence during years when stress is minimal.

Durable architecture is maintained not by reaction to crisis but by prevention of inward drift during calm.

Multi-Cycle Regime Modeling and Compounding Structural Divergence

The simulator begins by defining state variables at Year 0.

Reliable income floor is the statistically dependable annual inflow available under normal conditions without reliance on variable bonuses, speculative upside, or conditional performance components. Projected income includes contingent and cyclical components that may not persist across downturns.

Rigid load is the annualized sum of fixed and semi-fixed commitments that cannot be reduced within a short cycle without contractual friction or structural disruption. Margin ratio is the structural distance between reliable income floor and rigid load expressed as a proportion of reliable income.

Liquidity tiers are separated into operational liquidity, covering routine timing mismatches; tactical liquidity, covering moderate duration disturbances; and strategic liquidity, covering extended contraction scenarios. Liquidity runway is measured as the number of months rigid load can be supported if reliable income declines materially.

Obligation stacking density represents the proportion of reliable income pre-committed to rigid load. Duration stacking measures the overlap of long-term commitments that embed assumptions across multiple macro cycles.

Exposure concentration captures the degree to which income drivers, asset drivers, and sector risk are correlated. Asset convertibility defines the time and loss profile required to transform holdings into usable liquidity under stress.

Coupling density reflects the speed at which disturbance in one domain translates into pressure in others. Recovery velocity measures the number of cycles required to rebuild structural buffers after degradation.

Structural distance indicators are defined explicitly.

Distance to margin bypass equals reliable income floor minus rigid load. Distance to tier collapse equals liquidity runway minus expected contraction duration. Distance to forced asset conversion equals the time between liquidity depletion and obligation breach relative to asset conversion duration. Breakpoint migration direction is determined by whether these distances widen or narrow relative to operating baseline. Recovery velocity relative to disturbance frequency measures whether buffers rebuild faster than shocks recur.

These variables define the architecture.

PART 2

Two households begin with identical magnitudes. Each has a reliable income floor of $200,000. Each carries rigid load of $150,000. Each holds $600,000 in net worth. Macro conditions are stable. Asset markets are expanding moderately.

Household A structures obligations using projected income assumptions. Margin ratio relative to reliable floor is 12.5 percent. Liquidity tiers cover four months of rigid load. Tactical and strategic liquidity are not clearly separated. Obligation stacking density is high, with multiple long-duration commitments originated within a short period. Exposure concentration is elevated because primary income source and a significant portion of assets are tied to the same industry. Asset convertibility is limited due to real estate and employer equity concentration. Coupling density is high.

Household B structures obligations strictly relative to reliable floor. Margin ratio is 25 percent. Liquidity tiers cover ten months of rigid load with clear separation across operational, tactical, and strategic levels. Obligation durations are staggered deliberately across calendar years. Exposure concentration is moderate; asset drivers are partially independent of primary income source. Asset convertibility is aligned with volatility characteristics. Coupling density is lower.

At baseline, distance to margin bypass in Household A is $25,000. In Household B it is $50,000. Distance to tier collapse in Household A is approximately four months of rigid load. In Household B it is ten months. Distance to forced asset conversion is short in Household A due to limited runway and illiquidity alignment. In Household B it is materially longer.

Breakpoints in Household A sit near operating baseline. In Household B they sit further outward.

PART 3

Years 1 through 5 represent expansion.

Reliable income grows 5 percent annually. Projected income grows faster due to bonuses. Asset markets appreciate. Volatility remains suppressed.

In Household A, obligation scaling creep begins in Year 1. Additional housing commitments and long-duration service contracts are initiated using projected income growth. Margin ratio remains near 12 percent despite rising income because rigid load scales proportionately. Liquidity grows nominally but declines relative to rigid load as new commitments reduce surplus allocation to reserves. Asset appreciation concentrates further in employer equity and sector-specific investments.

Slack is converted into density.

By Year 3, obligation stacking density has increased. Duration layering intensifies as new commitments overlap existing ones. Liquidity runway relative to rigid load compresses to three months. Exposure concentration rises as appreciated assets form larger share of net worth.

Breakpoint migration is inward. Distance to margin bypass narrows relative to income volatility potential. Distance to tier collapse declines because rigid load grows faster than liquidity. Distance to forced asset conversion shortens as asset illiquidity increases relative to liquidity depth.

In Household B, income growth triggers governance scaling lag. Surplus widens margin ratio to 30 percent before new commitments are introduced. Liquidity tiers deepen to twelve months of rigid load. Asset appreciation is partially diversified into uncorrelated drivers. Obligation durations are staggered; no clustering occurs within a narrow time band.

Slack compounds.

Breakpoint migration is outward. Distance to margin bypass widens because rigid load grows more slowly than reliable income. Distance to tier collapse increases due to deeper runway. Asset convertibility remains aligned; distance to forced asset conversion lengthens.

Real-world density is visible without advisory framing. In Household A, bonus-based income is used to justify fixed-cost expansions such as larger mortgage commitments and multi-year service contracts initiated during high bonus years. In Household B, bonus income is allocated to liquidity tiers first, delaying commitment origination until buffer targets are exceeded.

By Year 5, surface metrics favor Household A in nominal net worth due to concentrated appreciation and larger asset positions. Structural distance favors Household B.

PART 4

Year 6 introduces moderate contraction.

Reliable income declines 18 percent due to sector slowdown. Projected income components disappear. Asset markets decline 20 percent, with heavier losses in the concentrated sector. Minor timing disruption delays income receipt for one cycle.

In Household A, distance to margin bypass collapses immediately. Rigid load now exceeds reliable income by a material margin. Margin bypass occurs in first contraction cycle. Operational liquidity absorbs timing mismatch but proves insufficient for sustained shortfall. Tactical reserves are engaged by Month 3. Because liquidity tiers are not clearly separated, tactical and strategic buffers blend quickly. Distance to tier collapse shrinks rapidly.

Asset volatility compounds stress. Correlated depreciation reduces net worth. Illiquidity prevents rapid conversion without loss. Distance to forced asset conversion narrows because liquidity runway is short and asset conversion requires extended timelines.

Propagation speed is high due to coupling density. Margin → liquidity → asset pressure occurs within two cycles. By Month 9, liquidity is near exhaustion. Obligation renegotiation becomes necessary.

In Household B, margin absorbs first several months of contraction. Distance to margin bypass remains positive due to widened ratio. Tactical liquidity is not activated until later in Year 6. Tier separation preserves strategic reserves. Asset volatility is partially offset by dispersion. Distance to forced asset conversion remains long because liquidity runway exceeds expected contraction duration.

Propagation is localized.

Containment sequencing remains intact: margin absorbs initial shock, tactical tier absorbs sustained shortfall, strategic tier remains untouched.

Breakpoint migration in Household A is inward; thresholds are crossed. In Household B thresholds are approached but not breached.

PART 5

Years 7 and 8 bring partial recovery.

Reliable income recovers to 92 percent of prior peak. Asset markets rebound modestly but volatility persists.

Household A begins recovery from compressed state. Liquidity tiers were depleted. Distance to tier collapse is near zero at beginning of recovery. Surplus under partial income restoration is thin because rigid load remains elevated. Recovery velocity is slow; rebuilding liquidity to four-month runway requires multiple cycles of disciplined surplus allocation. However, surplus is limited by obligation density. Asset base remains partially impaired due to prior forced liquidation.

Recovery inversion is visible. Degradation during contraction occurred within twelve months. Rebuilding to pre-contraction liquidity depth may require three to four years.

Household B begins recovery with intact strategic reserves. Tactical tier is partially reduced but operational liquidity stable. Surplus under partial income restoration is directed first to restoring tactical tier to pre-contraction depth. Recovery velocity is faster because degradation was limited. Within one year, liquidity tiers return to prior levels. Margin ratio widens again due to scaling lag.

Duration stacking in Household A persists; long-term commitments originated during expansion remain active. In Household B, staggered durations provide optional recalibration windows; some commitments mature during recovery, reducing rigid load.

Structural distance indicators diverge further. In Household A, distance to margin bypass remains narrow during recovery. In Household B, it widens beyond pre-contraction baseline.

PART 6

Year 9 introduces secondary disturbance before Household A completes rebuilding.

Income declines 10 percent for two consecutive years due to renewed sector weakness. Asset volatility resumes, though less severe than initial contraction.

Path dependence becomes decisive.

Household A enters second disturbance with shallow liquidity and narrow margin. Distance to margin bypass is minimal; margin bypass occurs immediately. Distance to tier collapse is short; tactical reserves deplete within months. Asset convertibility is impaired due to prior liquidation reducing liquid holdings. Forced asset conversion becomes likely to maintain obligations. Nonlinear escalation occurs as asset liquidation under moderate volatility realizes losses disproportionate to shock magnitude.

Threshold sensitivity has increased relative to first contraction. Smaller shock produces similar stress because buffers were not fully restored.

Household B enters second disturbance with rebuilt liquidity tiers and widened margin. Margin absorbs first months of contraction. Tactical tier engages late and remains above collapse threshold. Asset dispersion reduces correlated loss. No forced conversion is required.

Cumulative propagation in Household A results in structural erosion: reduced net worth, renegotiated obligations under constraint, compressed margin ratio, and elevated coupling density due to concentration of remaining assets.

Contained propagation in Household B preserves structure.

PART 7

Horizontal branching clarifies structural sensitivity.

Branch 1: Asset volatility precedes income contraction.

If asset markets decline 25 percent in Year 5 while income remains stable for six months before contracting, Household A experiences balance sheet erosion first. Exposure concentration magnifies net worth decline. Although margin remains temporarily intact, perceived wealth reduction may restrict credit flexibility and reduce psychological tolerance, but structurally the key effect is reduced distance to forced asset conversion before income decline. When income later contracts, liquidity tiers are already psychologically stressed, and asset base is weakened. Propagation accelerates because asset domain has been pre-compromised.

In Household B, asset volatility under dispersion reduces net worth modestly but does not impair liquidity alignment. Distance to forced asset conversion remains long. When income contraction follows, structural containment sequence remains orderly.

Branch 2: Governance intervention mid-expansion.

Assume Household A introduces scaling lag discipline in Year 3 after observing rising obligation density. Obligation scaling pauses for two years while liquidity deepens and asset dispersion increases modestly. Duration staggering is introduced for new commitments. As a result, breakpoint migration slows and partially reverses. When contraction arrives in Year 6, distance to margin bypass is slightly larger than in prior scenario, delaying liquidity activation by one or two cycles. Though still more fragile than Household B, the severity of compression reduces materially. Governance mid-cycle alters threshold migration direction.

Branch 3: Extended slow recovery.

Assume recovery from first contraction is slow, with income stagnating at 85 percent of prior peak for four years. Household A remains in compressed regime for extended period. Recovery velocity relative to disturbance frequency is negative; buffers rebuild slower than minor shocks recur. Even small expenses reactivate liquidity stress. Breakpoints remain proximate for years. Structural fatigue accumulates.

Household B under slow recovery experiences reduced surplus but maintains positive margin due to widened baseline. Liquidity rebuild slows but does not reverse. Threshold distance remains positive. Extended stagnation does not trigger nonlinear escalation because buffers were deeper at onset.

Each branch demonstrates that threshold migration direction determines sensitivity to shock ordering and recovery speed variation.

PART 8

Year 15 snapshot.

Reliable income for both households has returned to modest growth trajectory. Net worth differs due to realized losses and preserved compounding.

Household A exhibits margin ratio of 10 percent. Liquidity runway covers three to four months of rigid load. Obligation density remains high relative to reliable floor. Exposure concentration remains elevated because diversification was constrained by prior losses. Asset convertibility is limited. Distance to margin bypass is narrow; minor contraction would trigger liquidity activation quickly. Distance to tier collapse is short. Recovery velocity remains slower than potential disturbance frequency.

Household B exhibits margin ratio above 30 percent. Liquidity runway exceeds fifteen months of rigid load. Obligation density is proportionate to reliable floor with staggered durations. Exposure dispersion remains intact. Asset convertibility aligns with volatility band. Distance to margin bypass is wide. Distance to tier collapse is long. Recovery velocity exceeds disturbance frequency.

Compounding slack is visible in widened tolerance band. Compounding fragility is visible in compressed tolerance band.

The divergence arises solely from configuration choices across cycles.

Identical starting magnitudes produced materially different structural outcomes over fifteen years. Slack compounding widened breakpoints outward in one architecture. Fragility compounding migrated breakpoints inward in the other.

Coupling density governed propagation speed. Governance discipline governed breakpoint migration. Recovery velocity relative to disturbance frequency determined long-horizon optionality.

The system's durability was not determined by income magnitude, asset growth rate, or macro conditions alone. It was determined by how structural distances were widened or narrowed during expansion and how buffers were rebuilt or neglected during recovery.

Over multiple cycles, small configuration differences compounded into materially different tolerance regimes.

Structural divergence is cumulative.

The simulator concludes with two households of similar income but fundamentally different stability architecture.

The divergence is architectural, not arithmetic.

The fifteen-year snapshot captures divergence at a single point in time. The deeper structural implication emerges when examining not only static distances but trajectory momentum.

At Year 15, Household A is not merely closer to nonlinear thresholds. It is operating with inward migration momentum. Each incremental expansion phase tends to scale obligations before buffers widen meaningfully because prior compression reduced available surplus for disciplined retention. Liquidity rebuild is constrained by legacy commitments that were not fully recalibrated. Exposure concentration remains elevated because diversification requires capital allocation capacity that was eroded during forced liquidation cycles.

This creates a persistence bias toward fragility.

Distance to margin bypass remains narrow not only in magnitude but in trend. Even modest income growth tends to be absorbed by restoring lifestyle and servicing stacked commitments rather than widening structural distance. Liquidity tiers grow slowly relative to rigid load. Recovery velocity remains lower than disturbance frequency potential. Breakpoint migration remains inward-biased or, at best, static.

In contrast, Household B operates with outward migration momentum.

Because margin ratio widened materially during earlier expansion phases and was preserved through disciplined scaling lag, surplus capacity remains meaningful even after moderate contractions. Liquidity tiers, once rebuilt, provide cushion that allows growth to widen structural distance further without immediate obligation scaling. Exposure dispersion maintains asset convertibility alignment. Duration staggering continues to create recalibration windows across cycles.

Recovery velocity exceeds degradation velocity.

This asymmetry alters future cycle sensitivity. Even if both households face identical macro disturbances in Years 16–20, their structural response will diverge further.

If a new moderate contraction of 12 percent income occurs in Year 17, Household A will likely experience margin bypass within the first cycle due to narrow margin ratio. Liquidity activation will follow quickly because runway remains shallow. Asset conversion pressure will arise earlier because reserves are thin. Coupling density will again accelerate propagation.

Household B, entering the same contraction with wide margin and extended runway, will absorb shock within surplus for several cycles. Tactical tier may engage late. Strategic reserves remain insulated. Asset convertibility remains intact due to dispersion. Breakpoints remain distant.

Over twenty years, repeated moderate disturbances compound structural divergence.

The simulator also reveals second-order effects in obligation origination timing.

In Household A, commitments originated during expansion phases cluster within narrow calendar windows because scaling decisions follow income peaks. Mortgage refinances, long-term leases, vehicle financing, and service contracts tend to be executed during years of strong income and asset appreciation. This results in duration stacking density that embeds similar maturity dates across cycles. When recalibration windows arise, they do so simultaneously, increasing synchronization risk.

In Household B, duration staggering distributes maturity across years deliberately. Even if income declines, not all commitments lock in simultaneously. This creates structural flexibility at predictable intervals. Recalibration opportunities are embedded in architecture rather than forced by crisis.

Liquidity rebuild discipline also diverges in real-world density.

After contraction in Household A, liquidity rebuild competes with consumption restoration and asset repurchase. Surplus allocation tension is high. Because rigid load remains elevated, surplus available for buffer widening is limited. Liquidity rebuild sequencing may be incomplete before next disturbance occurs.

In Household B, liquidity rebuild sequencing is predefined. Operational tier is restored before tactical tier expansion. Tactical tier is restored before any increase in illiquid asset allocation. This sequencing preserves tier integrity and prevents premature recoupling.

Exposure dispersion further compounds divergence.

In Household A, sector concentration amplifies income and asset volatility synchrony. Each contraction erodes both domains concurrently. Rebuilding requires both income recovery and asset appreciation, which may not align temporally. This dual dependence slows recovery velocity.

In Household B, partial independence between income and asset drivers allows one domain to stabilize while the other contracts. Asset stability during income contraction extends runway. Income stability during asset volatility preserves margin. Cross-domain buffering reduces propagation speed.

Across decades, these structural differences alter optionality envelope.

Optionality envelope can be measured as the range of feasible responses available under disturbance without crossing nonlinear breakpoints. In Household A, the envelope narrows with each cycle because buffers erode faster than they rebuild. In Household B, the envelope widens because buffers rebuild faster than they erode.

Path dependence intensifies over time.

Because Household A experienced forced asset liquidation during secondary disturbance, its asset base composition permanently shifted toward reduced diversification and lower capital base. Even if income growth resumes, asset compounding occurs on smaller base. Liquidity rebuild remains constrained by reduced surplus. Obligation renegotiations during crisis may have extended duration of certain commitments, increasing rigidity density in later years.

In Household B, absence of forced liquidation preserved asset base. Asset compounding continues uninterrupted. Liquidity depth allows opportunistic asset acquisition during volatility without compromising structural distance. Duration staggering persists. Path dependence compounds resilience.

Shock ordering sensitivity also persists.

If a large asset volatility event precedes income contraction in Year 18, Household A's concentrated asset base may decline materially before income declines. Even if income remains stable temporarily, reduced net worth and illiquidity alignment shorten distance to forced asset conversion. When income contraction subsequently occurs, structural distance is already compressed. Household B, with dispersion and liquidity depth, remains insulated from early asset shock and enters income contraction from stronger baseline.

Recovery speed variation further differentiates long-horizon outcomes.

If macro recovery after Year 17 contraction is rapid, Household A may stabilize without full collapse but will likely rebuild slowly due to thin margin. Household B will widen margin rapidly because surplus re-expands and buffers were not exhausted deeply. If recovery is slow and prolonged, Household A remains in compression zone for extended duration, increasing probability of cumulative erosion. Household B, with deeper runway, can tolerate extended stagnation without crossing thresholds.

The simulator thus demonstrates not a single divergence event but a compounding structural separation across cycles.

By Year 20 or 25, magnitude differences become secondary to tolerance differences.

Household A may maintain similar nominal income and moderate net worth but operates perpetually near nonlinear zones. Every expansion phase risks recoupling because buffer rebuilding is incomplete. Every contraction phase threatens liquidity collapse because thresholds remain proximate.

Household B may maintain similar income magnitude but operates with wide tolerance band. Expansion widens slack before scaling. Contraction compresses slack but does not eliminate it. Recovery restores and extends structural distance.

Over decades, coupling compounds fragility through inward breakpoint migration. Decoupling compounds optionality through outward breakpoint migration.

The structural simulator does not require extreme shocks to generate divergence. Moderate, recurring disturbances are sufficient when coupling density is high and governance discipline is absent.

Identical starting income and net worth therefore do not determine long-horizon stability. Configuration decisions regarding margin ratio, liquidity tier depth, obligation stacking, exposure concentration, asset convertibility, and scaling lag determine threshold migration direction across time.

When breakpoints migrate inward across cycles, fragility compounds quietly during prosperity and accelerates during contraction.

When breakpoints migrate outward across cycles, optionality compounds quietly during prosperity and stabilizes contraction response.

The divergence is cumulative and time-amplified.

This completes the multi-cycle structural simulation.

Institutionalized Structural Audit and Threshold Governance

Reliable income floor is the lowest dependable inflow validated across prior cycles and stress conditions. Rigid load is the total annualized commitment structure that must be serviced independent of optimism. Margin ratio is the surplus between reliable income floor and rigid load expressed as a percentage of reliable floor. Liquidity tiers consist of operational liquidity for short-term sequencing, tactical liquidity for modeled contraction absorption, and strategic liquidity for multi-cycle endurance. Runway is the number of months of rigid load that total liquidity tiers can sustain under stress assumptions. Exposure concentration is the combined correlation overlap between income drivers and asset drivers. Duration stacking density measures the clustering of obligation maturities within defined time windows. Coupling density reflects translation speed between income, liquidity, asset, and obligation domains. Recovery velocity is the time required to restore structural buffers relative to disturbance frequency. Breakpoint migration refers to directional movement of nonlinear thresholds inward toward operating baseline or outward away from it.

I. Governance as Control System, Not Review

Structural drift occurs through incremental ratio changes. Rising income invites proportional scaling. Asset appreciation increases exposure concentration passively. Liquidity drawn for sequencing is not fully restored. Maturity clustering accumulates through convenience rather than design. None of these require error; they require time and absence of constraint.

Governance must therefore operate as a closed-loop control system. In a closed loop, structural outputs are continuously measured and compared to predefined bands. Deviations activate correction without discretionary delay. The system consists of sensors, actuators, and a clock cycle.

Sensors are structural distance metrics. Distance to margin bypass, distance to tier collapse, convertibility gap, concentration vector magnitude, duration clustering density, and recovery velocity ratio function as geometric measurements. They convert abstract stability into numerical distance.

Actuators are enforcement mechanisms. Scaling freeze halts rigid load growth. Surplus reallocation deepens liquidity tiers. Dispersion action reduces exposure concentration. Origination delay staggers duration clustering. Rigid load recalibration reduces structural density. These are not advisory suggestions; they are constraint responses triggered by ratio compression.

Clock cycle is cadence. Quarterly recalibration updates sensors and evaluates trigger conditions. Event-driven recalculation occurs when structure changes materially. Annual deep audit reassesses volatility band and correlation assumptions. Without clock cycle, closed loop degenerates into intermittent review, allowing drift to accumulate between measurements.

Governance as control system converts architecture into regulated geometry. Without it, geometry shifts invisibly until stressed.

II. Structural Distance Panel

Distance to margin bypass must be evaluated under multiple compression vectors.

Under rising income regimes, rigid load often scales with projected increases. Suppose reliable income floor increases from 220,000 to 260,000 over eight quarters. If rigid load increases from 165,000 to 215,000 during same period, margin ratio declines from 25 percent to 17 percent despite nominal surplus increase. Compression math reveals inward breakpoint migration even though income magnitude rises. Trend tracking across eight to ten quarters identifies slope of ratio change. A declining slope over consecutive quarters signals compression even before threshold breach.

Consider a second scenario: reliable floor rises from 300,000 to 345,000 over six quarters. Rigid load rises from 210,000 to 275,000 through housing upgrade and recurring service additions. Margin ratio declines from 30 percent to 20 percent. Nominal surplus rises from 90,000 to 70,000, but structural distance to bypass compresses by one-third.

In another case, reliable floor increases 8 percent annually while rigid load increases 11 percent annually. Over three years, margin ratio moves from 27 percent to 19 percent even though income and net worth both rise. Compression emerges from growth asymmetry rather than decline.

Trend behavior must distinguish level from slope and acceleration. If margin ratio declines from 28 percent to 26 percent to 24 percent to 23 percent across four quarters, slope negative and acceleration increasing. Even if absolute ratio remains above minimum band, acceleration indicates inward breakpoint migration likely to breach within projected two quarters absent intervention.

A household may report surplus rising from 50,000 to 65,000 annually, yet margin ratio declines from 22 percent to 16 percent because rigid load expansion outpaces reliable floor stability. Magnitude obscures geometry; distance shrinks beneath apparent improvement.

Under inflation regimes, nominal income and nominal rigid load may rise in parallel. If both increase 6 percent annually, nominal margin may appear constant. However, if liquidity tiers are not adjusted upward equivalently, runway measured in real purchasing power declines. Margin ratio in real terms compresses because real surplus growth may lag inflation-adjusted cost structure. Compression math must therefore incorporate real rigid load rather than nominal alone.

A second inflation example: reliable floor grows from 250,000 to 265,000 nominally while rigid load grows from 190,000 to 210,000 due to rent and insurance increases. Nominal margin remains 60,000, but margin ratio declines from 24 percent to 21 percent. Real purchasing power decline further compresses effective margin to 18 percent equivalent.

Another compression vector appears when healthcare or tax burdens rise disproportionately relative to income. Reliable floor remains static at 280,000 while rigid load increases 12,000 annually from mandatory cost increases. Margin ratio declines from 26 percent to 22 percent without discretionary scaling.

Trend behavior across eight to ten quarters under inflation shows flat nominal margin but declining real runway and rising rigid load percentage. Acceleration of decline visible when inflation persists longer than assumed.

Runway declines from 14 months to 11 months in real terms even though bank balances appear constant.

Under declining reliable floor scenarios, such as compensation mix shift or industry contraction, margin ratio can compress without new commitments. If reliable floor falls 12 percent while rigid load remains constant, margin ratio declines proportionally. Trend tracking must capture such exogenous compression and activate recalibration before rigid load becomes unsustainable.

For example, reliable floor drops from 320,000 to 280,000 due to bonus variability reclassification. Rigid load fixed at 230,000 shifts margin ratio from 28 percent to 18 percent instantly.

In a second case, reliable floor reduced from 240,000 to 220,000 while rigid load previously scaled to 195,000. Margin compresses from 18.7 percent to 11.3 percent, approaching bypass threshold rapidly.

Trend behavior in declining floor contexts often shows abrupt step compression rather than gradual slope. False stability may appear if projected income still exceeds prior totals, leading to assumption of safety despite reliable floor decline.

Distance to tier collapse compares runway to modeled contraction duration. Modeled contraction duration is derived from prior volatility patterns and stress calibration. If contraction assumption is nine months and runway twelve months, distance equals three months buffer. If liquidity partially used for discretionary purposes, runway may degrade to ten months. Degradation of two months reduces buffer to one month beyond contraction model. If subsequent minor drawdown reduces runway to eight months, tier collapse risk emerges because runway falls below contraction duration.

Consider runway initially 18 months against modeled contraction of 12 months. If rigid load increases by 10 percent while liquidity static, runway declines to 16 months. Subsequent discretionary use of 40,000 reduces runway to 14 months. Contraction duration assumption unchanged, buffer shrinks from six months to two months within one year.

Another case: runway 15 months, contraction modeled at 10 months. Tactical tier used for asset purchase reducing liquidity by 25 percent. Runway declines to 11 months. Simultaneous rigid load increase of 5 percent lowers runway further to 10 months. Buffer effectively eliminated though no contraction yet occurred.

Trend behavior shows runway erosion through small quarterly reductions: 17 months to 16 to 14.5 to 13. Acceleration when rigid load increases coincide with liquidity drawdowns.

False stability emerges when net worth increases due to asset appreciation while liquidity tiers shrink proportionally. Household appears wealthier; runway declines from 16 months to 11 months unnoticed.

Distance to forced asset conversion measures runway against convertibility lag under stress rather than calm. In calm markets, asset liquidation may require minimal time. Under stress, bid-ask spreads widen and transaction time increases. Convertibility lag must therefore be modeled under stress scenario. If illiquid assets require five months to convert under stress and runway equals four months, forced conversion probability increases. If correlated asset drawdown occurs simultaneously, asset value may decline before liquidation possible, compounding loss.

Consider illiquid real estate requiring six months under stress. Runway 7 months appears adequate. If contraction reduces income and minor liquidity use reduces runway to 5 months, convertibility lag exceeds runway, forcing distressed pricing.

In another example, private equity holdings with 12-month redemption restrictions combined with runway of 9 months create immediate forced conversion risk under income contraction.

Trend behavior may show convertibility lag increasing due to market conditions while runway constant. Distance shrinks invisibly.

Net worth improves; forced conversion risk unchanged or worse if appreciation concentrated.

Exposure concentration vector must capture passive appreciation drift. If sector allocation grows from 40 percent to 65 percent of net worth due to appreciation, concentration increases without transaction. Employer equity amplification occurs when compensation includes equity grants that accumulate over time, aligning income and asset drivers. Correlation stacking across accounts occurs when retirement accounts, brokerage accounts, and deferred compensation all hold similar sector exposures, multiplying concentration.

Additional example: income derived 80 percent from technology sector. Asset allocation initially 50 percent technology. Appreciation raises asset technology weight to 70 percent. Combined exposure exceeds 75 percent effective correlation.

Another scenario: two income earners both employed in same industry while majority of investments in industry ETF. Concentration index increases even if each component individually below threshold.

Trend behavior across 8–10 quarters may show concentration rising 3 percentage points per quarter due to appreciation. Acceleration indicates bubble-phase amplification.

False stability emerges when asset values increase significantly in concentrated sector, improving net worth and margin perception, while correlation risk intensifies.

Duration stacking density requires maturity histogram modeling. Obligations mapped across time reveal clustering risk. If 55 percent of long-term commitments mature within a 24-month window, synchronization risk high. Under contraction timing mismatch—contraction coinciding with clustered maturities—recalibration opportunity exists but liquidity may be constrained. If contraction occurs outside cluster, rigid load remains fixed longer, increasing stress duration. Histogram analysis must update as renewals and new commitments occur.

Second example: mortgage, vehicle loans, tuition commitments, and lease agreements all originated within two-year expansion. 60 percent of obligations mature between years 5 and 7. Clustered maturity amplifies refinancing risk.

Third scenario: staggered maturities at 3, 6, 9, and 12 years reduce clustering density below 30 percent in any 24-month band.

Trend behavior: gradual renewal of short-term obligations into identical durations re-creates clustering if not staggered intentionally.

Recovery velocity versus disturbance frequency requires multi-cycle compression math. If recovery from liquidity depletion requires 30 months and moderate disturbances occur every 48 months, positive velocity margin exists. If recovery requires 54 months and disturbances every 48 months, negative velocity scenario arises: buffers never fully restored before next shock. Multi-cycle modeling reveals compounding compression where each cycle begins from lower baseline. Negative velocity increases probability of tier collapse over time even if individual shocks moderate.

Additional example: disturbance every 36 months, recovery takes 40 months. Each cycle begins with 10 percent less liquidity than prior baseline. After three cycles, runway reduced from 14 months to 9 months.

Second example: recovery 24 months, disturbance frequency 60 months. Slack accumulates; runway increases from 12 months to 18 months across two cycles.

Trend behavior: recovery duration lengthening across cycles indicates fatigue.

A quarterly dashboard implementation collapses the panel into a small set of distances that are read the same way each cycle, with thresholds stated as bands rather than narrative interpretation: Margin ratio (target ≥ 25%), Runway months (target ≥ 14 months), Convertibility gap (stress lag ≤ runway minus 3 months), Concentration index (target ≤ 60%), Duration clustering (target ≤ 35% within next 24 months), Recovery velocity ratio (target ≥ 1.0, meaning rebuild time ≤ disturbance interval). Each quarterly cycle records current value, prior-quarter value, and the band status so that enforcement decisions are tied to the panel rather than to short-term context.

III. Embedded Gate Architecture

New obligation origination requires post-action recalculation of margin ratio, runway, concentration index, and duration clustering. Suppose proposed commitment adds 18,000 annual rigidity. Post-action margin ratio recalculated under reliable floor of 280,000 declines from 28 percent to 21 percent. If band floor is 25 percent, failure state triggered. Enforcement response: origination blocked or alternative rigid load reduction required before approval. If runway declines from 15 months to 12 months and band minimum 14 months, surplus reallocation must occur before commitment proceeds.

Offset pathway involves reducing existing rigid load by equivalent amount, deepening liquidity tiers by incremental surplus allocation, or staggering commitment start date until margin restored.

Sequencing rule requires recalculation first, offset identification second, approval only after ratio restored above band.

Failure mode if bypassed: margin compresses, reducing shock absorption capacity; subsequent minor contraction triggers bypass earlier than projected, activating liquidity tiers prematurely.

In a full commitment origination gate, the sequence is treated as a computation and an authorization, not a discussion. A proposed obligation adds 24,000 to annual rigid load. Pre-origination reliable floor is 300,000 and rigid load is 210,000, producing a margin ratio of 30 percent; liquidity tiers total 210,000 against monthly rigid load of 17,500, producing runway of 12 months. Post-origination rigid load becomes 234,000 and monthly rigid load becomes 19,500; margin ratio compresses to 22 percent and runway compresses to 10.8 months. Failure state is simultaneous: margin band breached and runway band breached. Offset plan must be specified in the same authorization packet: either remove 15,000 of existing annual rigidity and allocate 60,000 into liquidity tiers to restore runway above 14 months, or delay origination until surplus accumulation increases liquidity tiers by 70,000 while reducing rigid load growth to zero. Approval occurs only when post-offset recalculation restores margin ratio ≥ 25 percent and runway ≥ 14 months.

Renewal under changed reliable floor requires recalculation using updated floor. If reliable floor reduced from 300,000 to 260,000 and renewal maintains rigid load at 225,000, margin ratio falls from 25 percent to 13 percent. Failure state immediate. Enforcement response: renegotiation, downsizing, or concurrent rigid load reduction elsewhere before renewal permitted.

Offset pathway includes extending duration at lower annual cost, substituting flexible commitments, or reallocating surplus to rebuild margin before renewal.

Sequencing requires revalidation of reliable floor, recalculation of margin, evaluation of duration cluster impact, then decision.

Failure mode bypass leads to persistent compression and elevated risk of liquidity tier breach upon moderate income fluctuation.

Asset acquisition gate differentiates liquid and illiquid assets. For illiquid acquisition financed through liquidity tiers, runway recalculated post-acquisition. If liquidity reduced from 240,000 to 160,000 and rigid load 20,000 per month, runway declines from 12 months to 8 months. If contraction duration assumption 10 months, failure state. Enforcement response: acquisition delayed or liquidity restored through surplus accumulation before execution.

Offset pathway includes staged purchase, partial financing with liquidity preservation, or prior surplus allocation to tiers.

Sequencing requires liquidity deepening before asset transfer, not after.

Failure mode: reduced runway combined with income contraction forces distressed sale of newly acquired asset.

Exposure increase gate applies to correlated asset purchase or additional employer equity. Post-purchase concentration index recalculated. If overlap between income and asset drivers exceeds defined threshold—e.g., combined exposure surpasses 70 percent—failure state. Enforcement response: dispersion action required before additional correlated exposure allowed.

Offset pathway involves reallocating existing holdings to diversify drivers or hedging concentration through counter-correlated assets.

Sequencing requires concentration index recalculated before trade settlement.

Failure mode: correlated downturn simultaneously reduces income and asset value, amplifying forced conversion probability.

Tier drawdown event gate activates when tactical or strategic liquidity used. Post-drawdown runway recalculated. If runway falls below band, automatic rebuild schedule activated. Discretionary expenditures blocked until runway restored.

Offset pathway requires immediate surplus redirection to liquidity tiers and freeze on rigid load scaling.

Sequencing: drawdown logged, runway recalculated, rebuild schedule enforced before discretionary allocations resume.

Failure mode: repeated drawdowns without rebuild compress runway below contraction duration threshold.

Windfall event gate requires classification of inflow as non-recurring unless validated across cycles. Post-allocation margin and runway recalculated assuming windfall not added to reliable floor. If proposed rigid load scaling relies on windfall magnitude, failure state. Enforcement response: allocate windfall to liquidity tiers or rigid load reduction before any scaling.

Offset pathway includes splitting windfall across tiers and structural debt reduction.

Sequencing: classify, allocate to buffers, then evaluate structural scaling.

Failure mode: windfall converted into permanent rigid load increases, leading to margin compression once windfall absent.

Structural income increase event gate activates when reliable floor increases permanently. Post-increase margin ratio recalculated under unchanged rigid load. If margin ratio widens above upper band, scaling not automatic. Liquidity tiers must first widen proportionally to new rigid load multiples before new commitments approved. Enforcement response: staged scaling after buffer widening.

Offset pathway includes automatic surplus routing to liquidity tiers until runway reaches new target multiple.

Sequencing: validate permanence, widen buffers, then authorize scaled commitments.

Failure mode: immediate rigid load scaling eliminates newly created margin and reduces distance to bypass before next contraction.

IV. Cadence Integrity and Drift Detection

Quarterly recalibration mechanics require updating all structural distances using current data. Ratio trends plotted across prior quarters reveal directional migration. If margin ratio slope negative over three consecutive quarters, early drift signal emerges even if ratio within band.

Annual volatility band reassessment recalculates reliable floor based on trailing adverse quarters. If compensation variability increased or industry cyclicality changed, volatility band widened. Structural distance targets adjusted accordingly.

Structural regime shift detection examines persistent deviation in income volatility, convertibility timelines, or asset correlation patterns. For example, regulatory change increasing illiquidity of certain assets constitutes regime shift requiring immediate recalibration of convertibility lag and runway targets.

Threshold erosion detection monitors changes to band definitions themselves. If margin ratio band lowered from 25 percent to 20 percent without structural justification, meta-governance flag triggered. Governance override control protocol requires documentation of deviation reason, duration, and restoration plan. Overrides time-limited and cannot overlap without board-level review within governance framework.

Threshold drift detection compares current threshold values to original doctrine baseline. Any reduction in required runway multiple or increase in allowable concentration index must be justified by permanent structural change, not short-term comfort.

Second-order governance ensures that enforcement parameters do not erode silently and that drift in rules is identified before drift in ratios becomes irreversible.

V. Multi-Cycle Stress Integration

Asset shock precedes income shock. Correlated asset decline reduces net worth and liquidity confidence. First breakpoint stressed is convertibility gap if concentration high. Asset drawdown reduces collateral value and increases correlation vector magnitude. Propagation path: asset decline compresses strategic tier; liquidity fear leads to premature tactical use; income shock follows, stressing margin ratio. Concentration trigger during appreciation phase would have limited exposure and preserved convertibility distance, reducing initial compression.

Income shock precedes asset shock. Margin ratio stressed first. Reduced reliable floor compresses surplus; liquidity tiers activated. If margin band maintained, contraction absorbed locally. If compressed previously, bypass occurs immediately. Asset shock then interacts with depleted liquidity and increased concentration. Margin band trigger during expansion would have preserved first buffer and slowed translation speed.

High shock density scenario: two moderate contractions within three years. First contraction reduces runway from 15 months to 9 months. Recovery begins but velocity insufficient; runway only rebuilt to 11 months before second contraction reduces to 6 months. Propagation crosses tier collapse threshold; forced conversion risk rises. Recovery velocity trigger requiring rebuild to pre-shock plus strengthening before scaling would have maintained runway above 13 months, preserving distance.

Long calm expansion drift: eight-year low volatility period. Margin ratio declines gradually from 30 percent to 20 percent; concentration rises from 50 percent to 72 percent; runway declines from 18 to 12 months. No stress visible. Contraction then triggers simultaneous margin bypass and concentration amplification. Quarterly dispersion and scaling freeze triggers would have arrested drift at early slope inflection.

Structural regime change: volatility increases permanently due to industry disruption. Reliable floor recalculated downward 15 percent. Margin and runway insufficient under new assumptions. Propagation path: outdated volatility band underestimates contraction duration; tier collapse threshold misaligned. Annual volatility reassessment would have recalibrated contraction model and widened buffers before disruption intensified.

Inflation compression branch: persistent 7 percent inflation for four years. Rigid load escalates; liquidity nominally constant; real runway declines from 14 to 9 months. Contraction coinciding with inflation spike amplifies stress. Real-term recalibration trigger increasing liquidity targets annually would have preserved runway above contraction duration threshold.

In a two-shock density sequence with explicit timing, Shock A occurs in Quarter 1 with a 15 percent reliable floor contraction and a three-month timing disruption that draws down liquidity, moving runway from 14 months to 10 months and compressing margin ratio from 26 percent to 20 percent; recovery begins but recovery velocity implies 30 months to restore runway to 14 months. By Quarter 5, only partial rebuild has occurred and runway is 12 months when Shock B arrives, producing an additional 10 percent floor contraction and pushing runway to 8 months while moving margin ratio to 16 percent; breakpoint migration is inward across the sequence because the second disturbance lands inside the rebuild interval, and the tier collapse threshold shifts closer to baseline due to reduced distance and slowed recovery.

VI. Complexity Scaling and System Persistence

As architecture scales, dashboard compression logic aggregates multiple variables into simplified indicators without losing fidelity. Margin ratio, runway multiple, concentration index, clustering density, and recovery velocity displayed simultaneously to prevent siloed decision-making. A concrete dashboard panel displays: reliable floor (rolling 12-quarter minimum), rigid load (annualized), margin ratio percentage, runway months at current rigid load, contraction duration assumption, convertibility lag under stress, concentration index percentage, duration cluster percentage within next 24 months, recovery months required, disturbance frequency average.

Data integrity failure example occurs when projected bonus included in reliable floor classification, inflating margin ratio artificially from 22 percent to 29 percent. Subsequent bonus shortfall reduces reliable floor, compressing margin abruptly.

Tier-blending detection example: operational liquidity falls below two months while tactical tier remains high; discretionary expense drawn from tactical instead of restoring operational. Detection rule flags imbalance when operational < defined minimum regardless of total liquidity.

Structural change events triggering event-driven audit include: income source change, obligation origination above 5 percent rigid load, asset acquisition exceeding 10 percent net worth, regulatory change affecting liquidity, industry concentration shift, family structure change affecting rigid load, significant tax law change affecting reliable floor classification.

Automation ensures recalculation at each event; manual oversight insufficient at scale.

Governance under lifecycle shift requires recalibrating reliable floor trajectory as career transitions from growth to plateau. Rigid load must decline relative to floor before income declines. Liquidity tiers must increase as recovery velocity potential declines with reduced earning horizon.

Governance under intergenerational transfer requires documentation and dashboard continuity so successor decision-makers inherit ratios and triggers, not merely asset balances.

Structural fatigue arises when architecture operates near threshold for prolonged periods. Even without breach, repeated near-compression reduces optionality. Structural inertia modeling recognizes that larger rigid load and illiquid assets increase time required for correction. Early enforcement reduces inertia accumulation and prevents cumulative geometry distortion.

VII. Outward Breakpoint Migration as Permanent Policy

Post-recovery strengthening requirement mandates that after contraction buffers are restored beyond pre-shock baseline before any scaling resumes. Restoration to baseline insufficient because baseline may have been compressed. Strengthening widens margin and runway beyond prior levels, creating cumulative outward migration. Strengthening target logic requires margin ratio restored to prior baseline plus additional 3–5 percentage points and runway extended by minimum three additional months beyond prior pre-shock level before new commitments authorized.

Across 20–25 years, enforced architecture may widen margin ratio from 25 percent to 32 percent and deepen runway from 12 months to 20 months while maintaining concentration index below 60 percent. Unenforced architecture may see margin decline from 25 percent to 15 percent and runway from 12 months to 7 months while concentration rises above 75 percent.

Exposure concentration remains within band despite appreciation cycles under enforcement; duration clustering maintained below 35 percent within any 24-month window. Recovery velocity remains positive relative to disturbance frequency. Breakpoints migrate outward across cycles, increasing structural distance.

Unenforced architecture oscillates around shrinking margin and runway. Exposure concentration rises during appreciation and rarely corrected. Duration clustering accumulates. Recovery velocity declines. Breakpoints migrate inward gradually, then abruptly during stress.

Geometry divergence between enforced and unenforced architecture determines nonlinear response under severe disturbance. Outward migration increases optionality envelope; inward migration compresses it and narrows response domain.

FINAL DOCTRINE

Drift is continuous and geometric.
Governance must be continuous and mechanical.
Stability is enforced through ratios, gates, cadence, and recalculation.
Optionality is measurable structural distance preserved across cycles.
Breakpoint migration direction is determined by disciplined enforcement, not income magnitude.

Structural Trajectory and the Optionality Envelope

I. Architecture Determines Trajectory

Income magnitude does not determine long-horizon stability. Asset appreciation does not determine long-horizon stability. Configuration determines breakpoint migration. Breakpoint migration determines the optionality envelope. The optionality envelope determines life trajectory.

Breakpoint migration is not a metaphor. It is the observed movement of structural thresholds relative to baseline operating conditions. A system that migrates thresholds outward increases the range of variance it can absorb without structural damage. A system that migrates thresholds inward increases the probability that ordinary variance will cross a nonlinear boundary. The distinction is not whether bills are paid in a given month. The distinction is whether the system's tolerance distance is widening or narrowing across cycles.

Structural trajectory is the slope of breakpoint migration across time. A positive slope indicates outward migration. A negative slope indicates inward migration. Trajectory is measured in ratios and time tolerances, not in nominal dollars. A system can accumulate a higher nominal surplus while its trajectory remains negative if rigid load and exposure concentration rise faster than dependable capacity and buffer depth.

The two-household model provides a controlled baseline. Both households begin with identical income, identical net worth, identical macro conditions, and identical obligation magnitude. They differ only in configuration. Household A is configured with high coupling density, shallow liquidity, high stacking, correlated assets, and obligations scaled with projected income. Household B is configured with decoupled drivers, wider margin ratio, tier integrity, duration staggering, governance scaling lag, and dispersed asset drivers. These are not preferences. They are architectural decisions that determine tolerance geometry.

Extending horizon to 25–30 years shifts the analysis from event outcomes to trajectory outcomes. Over a single year, many configurations appear equivalent. Over a decade, differences in threshold distance become measurable. Over 25 years, small differences in ratio discipline compound into distinct option sets.

Model inward migration as a repeated compression of margin ratio. Suppose Household A experiences 5 percent inward margin compression per cycle over four macro cycles. The compression can be expressed as percentage point decline in margin ratio, not as nominal margin dollars. If Household A begins with a margin ratio of 25 percent relative to reliable floor, a 5 percent inward compression per cycle reduces that ratio by 1.25 percentage points each cycle. After four cycles, margin ratio is approximately 20 percent if no offsets occur. That may still appear functional in a calm period, but it materially shortens distance to margin bypass under contraction.

Runway erosion compounds similarly. Suppose Household A experiences 3-month runway erosion per contraction event through tier drawdown that is not fully rebuilt before scaling resumes. If runway begins at 14 months, four contractions reduce runway to 2 months below baseline if each erosion is permanent, leaving 2 months of runway at the end of the fourth cycle under constant rigid load assumptions. In practice rigid load typically rises, making runway erosion steeper. The path matters more than the endpoint; runway shrinking increases the likelihood of tier collapse during intermediate years when shocks occur.

Recovery velocity relative to disturbance frequency defines whether erosion is recoverable. If the system requires 36 months to rebuild its buffers after each contraction, but disturbances arrive every 30 months in clustered regimes, recovery is structurally incomplete when the next disturbance arrives. That condition produces cumulative inward migration even if each individual disturbance is moderate. The system begins each new contraction with reduced distance.

Contrast an outward-migrating configuration. Model Household B as widening margin ratio by 2 percent per cycle. If margin ratio begins at 25 percent and expands by 0.5 percentage points each cycle, after four cycles it reaches approximately 27 percent. This change appears small, but it is structural distance measured against a reliable floor that likely rises across decades. The widening ratio increases the absolute surplus distance between dependable capacity and rigid load.

Now add runway strengthening. Suppose Household B adds 2 months of runway post-recovery as a governance requirement before any new rigidity is originated. If runway begins at 14 months, after four cycles runway reaches 22 months assuming consistent strengthening and stable rigid load ratio. That difference is not cosmetic. It changes whether a second shock arriving before full recovery forces asset conversion or remains contained inside liquidity tiers.

These numerical examples are not forecasts. They show how small differences in migration direction, repeated across cycles, produce different tolerance geometry. Return differences can be offset by one forced conversion event. Ratio differences cannot be offset by one good year if enforcement is absent.

The compounding effect is structural rather than arithmetic. A 10 percent increase in income may raise surplus dollars. But if rigid load increases 8 percent and liquidity increases 2 percent, the architecture does not become more tolerant. It becomes denser. The system becomes more fragile despite higher magnitude.

Trajectory is therefore not an outcome. It is a configuration behavior across time. A household that treats growth as permission to convert slack into density produces negative slope even during prosperity. A household that treats growth as an opportunity to widen distance produces positive slope even when returns are modest. The slope, over 25–30 years, dominates the option set available at each decision point.

II. The Optionality Envelope Across Decades

Optionality envelope is the range of decisions available without crossing nonlinear thresholds. It is not a subjective sense of freedom. It is a measurable domain bounded by distance to margin bypass, distance to tier collapse, distance to forced asset conversion, and distance to obligation renegotiation. Optionality exists when decisions can be made without triggering threshold mechanisms. Optionality decays when decisions require threshold interaction to remain solvent.

Across 30 years, Household A's envelope narrows not through one catastrophic event but through repeated micro-compressions that increase sensitivity. High coupling density translates disturbances quickly. Shallow liquidity causes early activation. High stacking creates synchronization stress. Correlated assets introduce simultaneous income and asset vulnerability. Obligations scaled to projected income reduce margin distance and increase rigidity percentage.

As the envelope narrows, the system becomes increasingly sensitive to ordinary variance. Small disruptions activate liquidity tiers earlier. Sequencing mismatches become more consequential. The system begins to rely on tactical reserves to maintain continuity. Once tactical reserves are used for non-contraction purposes, runway shortens and the envelope tightens further. Forced renegotiations become more common because rigidity cannot be recalibrated quickly. Geographic flexibility declines because relocation costs and timing become difficult to absorb. Career mobility declines because transition periods require buffer depth, and buffer depth is missing. Each disturbance imposes higher structural cost because absorption occurs closer to breakpoints.

Household B's envelope widens through outward breakpoint migration. Disturbances are contained locally. Liquidity activation occurs later and at lower intensity. No forced liquidation occurs because convertibility lag remains inside runway distance. Optionality is not risk aversion; it is the capacity to take voluntary risk without being forced by system stress. Household B can accept temporary income reductions, relocate if necessary, or shift sectors without triggering nonlinear damage. It can withstand stagnation regimes because runway is deep and rigid load proportionate. It can absorb inflation regimes because liquidity and margin are not fully utilized by commitments.

Optionality compounds geometrically when slack compounds. Each cycle that ends with increased margin ratio and increased runway expands decision space in the next cycle. Fragility compounds geometrically when density compounds. Each cycle that ends with higher rigidity percentage, shorter runway, and higher concentration shrinks decision space. The shrinking domain increases the probability that future decisions are constrained by near-term cash requirements rather than multi-cycle coherence.

A 30-year horizon must include branching paths. Consider a career disruption in Year 18. The event is not the same as a single-year income decline. It includes transition time, possible geographic relocation, skill reallocation, and compensation re-stabilization. Household A enters Year 18 with narrowed envelope. Margin ratio has drifted downward. Runway has eroded through prior partial drawdowns. Exposure concentration remains high due to sector dominance. Duration stacking persists because long commitments were originated during expansion and renewed automatically.

Career disruption triggers immediate reliance on liquidity tiers. If disruption coincides with sector downturn, income contraction and asset drawdown are correlated. Tactical liquidity is activated early. If runway is insufficient relative to transition duration, convertibility pressure rises. Household A may be forced to sell assets during drawdown or renegotiate obligations. Either outcome imposes structural damage and increases coupling density because future options become constrained by the consequences of forced conversion.

Household B enters Year 18 with wider envelope. Margin ratio has migrated outward modestly but persistently. Runway is deep. Exposure is dispersed across drivers. Duration maturities are staggered, creating recalibration windows. Career disruption activates tactical liquidity but does not collapse it. Transition duration remains within runway. Asset holdings are not forced into conversion because convertibility lag remains inside buffer. The event is absorbed without structural damage, preserving optionality for the post-transition period.

Now model a health shock in Year 22. Health shocks combine cost increase and income volatility. They also impose time constraints and may alter the reliable floor permanently. Household A, already operating near thresholds, experiences immediate margin bypass risk due to cost surge. Liquidity is depleted faster than modeled because costs may be front-loaded. If prior career disruption forced liquidation, asset base is smaller and more concentrated, increasing fragility. The health shock interacts with structural fatigue. Correction time increases because the system has less slack and higher inertia.

Household B, with preserved buffer geometry, absorbs the health shock through operational and tactical tiers. If reliable floor declines permanently, obligations remain proportionate enough to allow recalibration without crisis. Asset conversion is avoidable because runway provides time. The event reduces optionality temporarily but does not collapse it.

Extended stagnation regime is another branch. Suppose Years 12–17 feature flat real income growth, modest volatility, and low asset appreciation. Household A's architecture depends on growth to sustain scaling decisions made earlier. Without growth, compression becomes visible: rigid load fixed, but reliable floor does not rise, so margin ratio does not widen. Liquidity rebuild is slow, so runway remains shallow. Even without a shock, optionality narrows because the system cannot regenerate slack. When the next disturbance occurs, threshold proximity is higher.

Household B does not require growth to maintain stability because governance preserves margin and runway as policy rather than as surplus residue. Stagnation is absorbed as a regime rather than as an event. Optionality does not expand rapidly, but it does not collapse because distance remains adequate. The system can remain in low-growth conditions without structural degradation.

Inflation spike regime is another branch. Inflation increases rigid load and reduces real liquidity value. Household A, with shallow runway, experiences rapid erosion of time tolerance. If obligations are fixed in nominal terms but discretionary costs rise, operational liquidity becomes unstable. Tactical tiers may be used to bridge purchasing power loss, creating tier blending. Inflation then functions as a slow contraction, compressing distance until a shock triggers collapse. Household B, with deeper runway and stronger margin, preserves time tolerance longer and can adjust without crossing thresholds. The optionality envelope narrows under inflation, but not to the point of forced conversion.

The divergence is not moral or psychological. It is mechanical. Optionality is a consequence of preserved structural distance. When distance is preserved, decisions remain within internal control. When distance is lost, decisions are forced by thresholds.

III. Ordering Sensitivity and Regime Shifts

Shock ordering matters because translation speed between domains is not symmetric. Some shocks first stress assets, others stress income, others stress obligations through inflation or rate resets, others stress liquidity through sequencing mismatch. Inward migration increases sensitivity to shock order because the system has reduced buffer distance and fewer intermediate absorption stages. Outward migration reduces ordering sensitivity because multiple buffers remain intact and can absorb disturbance regardless of entry point.

Branch A: Asset shock → Income shock → Slow recovery. Asset shock first stresses exposure concentration and convertibility lag. If assets draw down, strategic liquidity may be indirectly affected if it is stored in correlated instruments. If exposure concentration is high, asset shock also signals probable income shock because the same sector weakness affects employment or client demand. If recovery is slow, recovery velocity may fall below disturbance frequency, prolonging threshold proximity.

In an inward-migrated system, asset shock consumes optionality quickly. Liquidity may be used to avoid selling assets into drawdown, shortening runway. When income shock follows, margin bypass occurs earlier because rigid load was scaled under projected income assumptions. Slow recovery extends the time spent near thresholds, increasing structural fatigue and raising probability of forced renegotiation. In an outward-migrated system, asset shock is absorbed with less translation into liquidity because concentration is lower and runway deeper. Income shock arrives, but margin ratio remains adequate, and slow recovery does not cause cascade because recovery velocity remains above disturbance frequency.

Branch B: Income shock → Asset shock → Rapid recovery. Income shock first stresses margin ratio and operational liquidity. Asset shock later stresses net worth and convertibility but may occur after some buffer has already been used. Rapid recovery reduces time near thresholds. Inward systems fail because income shock triggers early tier activation; assets then draw down when liquidity is already depleted, forcing conversion. Outward systems contain income shock within margin and tactical tiers, preserving liquidity so asset shock does not force sale. Rapid recovery restores buffers before the next disturbance, allowing outward migration to continue.

Branch C: High-frequency moderate shocks. These are not severe events but clustered disturbances that arrive before full rebuild. The primary determinant here is recovery velocity relative to disturbance frequency. Inward systems with slow recovery accumulate erosion; each shock starts closer to thresholds. Outward systems with enforced post-shock strengthening rebuild faster and may even widen distance after each hit.

Branch D: Long calm expansion → sudden severe contraction. Long calm expansion increases drift risk. Inward systems convert slack into density and allow concentration to rise. Sudden contraction reveals hidden compression. The system may appear stable until contraction crosses thresholds rapidly. Outward systems use calm expansion to widen distance and disperse exposure. When severe contraction arrives, absorption occurs across multiple buffers, reducing need for forced conversion.

Regime shifts amplify ordering sensitivity because assumptions become obsolete. A regime shift may increase volatility, reduce reliable floor permanence, increase convertibility friction, or alter correlation structure between income and assets. Inward-migrated systems are brittle under regime shift because they have no slack to absorb model error. Outward-migrated systems can tolerate assumption error because distance is larger than the model required.

Structural fatigue is not emotion. It is the mechanical consequence of operating near thresholds over extended periods. When near thresholds, the system must allocate surplus to immediate stabilization rather than to strengthening. Correction time increases because each small disturbance consumes buffer. Illiquid density increases inertia; converting illiquidity to liquidity under stress requires time and incurs discount. Large rigid load increases reversal friction; obligations cannot be reduced quickly without renegotiation cost. Fatigue increases the probability that ordering sensitivity becomes decisive: a shock sequence that would have been tolerable in a rested system becomes destabilizing in a fatigued one.

Ordering sensitivity therefore functions as a multiplier. As migration moves inward, shock order increasingly determines whether the system can remain within buffers or crosses into threshold behavior. As migration moves outward, shock order matters less because distance absorbs variance from multiple entry points.

IV. Structural Momentum

Structural momentum is the tendency of systems to continue moving in their current migration direction. Momentum emerges from reinforcement loops embedded in configuration. An inward-biased system continues compressing during expansion because scaling decisions are made with projected income, liquidity is treated as deployable capital rather than as tolerance distance, and appreciation reinforces concentration. Outward-biased systems continue widening during expansion because governance requires buffer widening before scaling, and dispersion rules counteract passive drift.

Household A's growth is consumed restoring prior compression. When a contraction draws down liquidity, recovery is slow because rigid load remains high and surplus is limited by commitments. Growth that arrives during expansion is absorbed by obligations initiated during prior years. Liquidity rebuild remains partial because scaling resumes before buffers are restored. Obligations persist because duration stacking locks assumptions across cycles. Momentum remains inward because every expansion phase is used to reconstitute the same density that caused compression. Even when income rises, the system cannot widen distance because new rigidity absorbs the widening. Breakpoints migrate inward despite prosperity.

Household B's growth widens structural distance. After contraction, governance requires restoration plus strengthening, so expansion surplus is routed to tier deepening and margin widening before obligations scale. Liquidity deepens beyond prior peak, not merely back to baseline. Obligations are staggered deliberately; renewals are timed to avoid clustering. Exposure is moderated through dispersion actions that offset appreciation drift. Momentum remains outward because each expansion phase is used to increase tolerance distance rather than to increase density. The system accumulates slack as a structural feature.

Momentum alters future cycle sensitivity even if income is identical because it determines starting distance at the onset of each cycle. Two systems with identical income and net worth at Year 12 can diverge sharply by Year 18 because one enters contraction with deep runway and wide margin while the other enters with compressed buffers. Momentum also alters recovery dynamics: inward momentum systems devote recovery surplus to preventing immediate threshold breach, while outward momentum systems can allocate surplus to strengthening, reducing future sensitivity.

Momentum is also visible in threshold migration during calm. In inward systems, calm does not increase distance; it reduces it through density accumulation. In outward systems, calm increases distance because governance policies are enforced independent of volatility environment.

Over decades, momentum becomes structural inheritance. It determines whether the default state is near thresholds or far from them. It determines whether disturbances are manageable deviations or existential compressions. Momentum is therefore not a byproduct; it is a configuration outcome.

V. Stability Versus Wealth

Magnitude illusion is the belief that higher net worth implies higher stability. A system can have higher net worth and lower stability. A system can have lower net worth and higher optionality. Stability is determined by structural distance, not by asset magnitude. Wealth can be concentrated, illiquid, and correlated with income, producing high exposure concentration and high convertibility friction. Optionality requires liquidity and margin, which may reduce peak returns but preserve tolerance distance.

Two 30-year outcomes illustrate the divergence.

Household A experiences higher early asset growth due to concentrated exposure during favorable regime. Net worth rises quickly from appreciation, and confidence increases. Rigid load scales with projected income. Liquidity tiers shrink relative to obligations because capital is deployed into assets and commitments. Exposure concentration increases due to passive appreciation and employer equity accumulation. When a mid-cycle contraction occurs, the system requires liquidity to service rigid load. Liquidity is insufficient, and asset conversion becomes necessary. The conversion occurs under drawdown, realizing nonlinear loss. Loss realization reduces net worth and often increases future rigidity because obligations persist while asset base shrinks. Terminal net worth after 30 years may be lower than peak trajectory would suggest because forced liquidation creates permanent capital loss and reduces compounding base. The optionality envelope remains compressed because buffers were not preserved.

Household B experiences slower early growth due to dispersed exposures and liquidity retention. Net worth increases at a steadier rate, sometimes lagging concentrated peers during bull regimes. Liquidity tiers remain intact and are strengthened post-recovery. Exposure concentration is moderated, reducing correlation between income and asset drawdown. When contraction occurs, no forced liquidation is required because runway covers contraction duration and convertibility lag. Assets are retained through drawdowns and recover over time. The avoidance of forced conversion preserves the compounding base. Terminal net worth after 30 years can exceed Household A's despite lower early growth because the system avoids nonlinear loss realization and preserves capital through adverse regimes. The optionality envelope expands because distance is preserved and increased.

Avoidance of forced conversion compounds more than maximizing peak return because forced conversion introduces a discontinuity. Returns are continuous compounding in favorable periods. Forced conversion is a discrete event that resets compounding base lower. Over decades, one forced conversion can dominate years of incremental return advantage. The architecture that prevents forced conversion may appear conservative in calm regimes but produces superior retained capital and superior optionality under variance.

Stability versus wealth is therefore not a philosophical preference. It is a recognition that compounding requires survival through drawdowns without forced sale. Liquidity retention dampens fragility by extending time tolerance. Concentration-driven wealth amplifies fragility by aligning losses across domains. The system's outcome is determined by whether it can remain in the market and in its obligations without crossing nonlinear thresholds.

A higher net worth system with low runway and high concentration has a narrow optionality envelope. A lower net worth system with deep runway and dispersed drivers has a wider optionality envelope. The envelope determines what decisions remain voluntary versus forced.

VI. Governance Permanence

Drift is continuous. Governance must be continuous. This is not a motivational statement. It is a structural property of complex systems. Without enforcement, ratios drift toward compression because scaling incentives are asymmetric: expanding commitments provides immediate utility while buffer accumulation provides delayed utility. Asset appreciation creates passive concentration. Duration stacking accumulates as renewals occur. Liquidity is used for intermediate needs and not fully restored. Absent enforcement, these movements are not corrected.

If enforcement weakens, margin compresses. Runway shortens. Concentration rises. Duration clusters. Velocity slows. Breakpoints migrate inward. These are not independent. They reinforce each other.

Margin compression increases reliance on liquidity tiers. Liquidity tier use shortens runway. Short runway increases probability of forced conversion under stress. Forced conversion reduces asset base, slowing recovery. Slow recovery reduces ability to rebuild liquidity before next disturbance. Concentration amplifies income and asset correlation, making shocks simultaneous. Duration clustering limits recalibration windows, increasing rigidity during contractions.

If enforcement persists, margin widens. Runway deepens. Exposure disperses. Duration staggers. Velocity improves. Breakpoints migrate outward. This is also a coupled system. Margin widening reduces liquidity activation frequency. Reduced activation preserves runway. Preserved runway prevents forced conversion. Prevented conversion preserves asset base, improving recovery. Improved recovery allows strengthening beyond baseline before scaling resumes. Exposure dispersion reduces correlation between income and asset drawdowns, slowing translation speed. Duration staggering creates recalibration windows, reducing synchronization sensitivity.

Over 25 years, enforcement versus non-enforcement produces divergence even if average income and average return are similar. The enforced system accumulates distance. The unenforced system accumulates density. The divergence appears in the optionality envelope: ability to change careers, relocate, absorb health costs, withstand stagnation, and tolerate inflation regimes without crossing thresholds. The difference is not whether the household experiences shocks. Both do. The difference is whether shocks propagate into structural damage.

Governance permanence requires that enforcement operates during calm. Calm is when drift accumulates. During calm, the system has surplus and time, making buffer strengthening feasible. If enforcement is suspended during calm because risk appears low, inward migration accelerates. Stress survivability is determined by calm-phase governance, not by crisis-phase reaction.

Permanence also requires that governance is not reduced to intent. It must be procedural. Ratios must be measured on schedule. Triggers must operate automatically. Originations must pass gates. Overrides must be constrained. The purpose is not to prevent variance but to prevent variance from translating into threshold breach.

The long-horizon variable is breakpoint migration direction. Enforcement is the mechanism that controls that direction. Without enforcement, direction defaults inward. With enforcement, direction can be maintained outward.

VII. Long-Horizon Closure

Stability is architecture. Architecture is governed. Governance determines breakpoint migration. Breakpoint migration determines optionality. Optionality determines life trajectory.

Over decades, small differences in configuration compound more than income. A household that begins with a modestly wider margin ratio and a modestly deeper runway can end with a materially larger option set because each cycle ends with preserved distance rather than accumulated compression. A household that begins with high income and high asset growth can end with a narrower option set if it converts slack into density and allows correlation to rise, because the system's migration direction becomes inward.

Architecture compounds more than return rate because the return rate operates inside the constraints of the architecture. Return cannot compensate for forced conversion when conversion occurs at the wrong time. Return cannot compensate for obligation rigidity when rigidity forces liquidity activation. Return cannot compensate for recovery velocity when rebuild time exceeds disturbance frequency.

Stability compounds more than optimism because stability is not a belief. It is the repeated preservation of distance to nonlinear thresholds. It is the repeated separation of domains so disturbances do not translate instantly across the system. It is the repeated rebuilding of buffers faster than the environment can deplete them.

Over decades, configuration compounds more than income. Architecture compounds more than return rate. Stability compounds more than optimism.

Stability compounds more than optimism because optimism does not alter structural distance. Over long horizons, optimism often accelerates inward migration by relaxing enforcement during calm, allowing density to accumulate until thresholds are close enough that the next disturbance forces irreversible actions. The system does not fail because conditions become unusually hostile. It fails because its tolerance geometry was consumed while conditions were benign.

The optionality envelope is the only long-horizon output that matters mechanically, because it determines whether the system can respond to variance with discretionary choice or only with constraint-driven action. A widening envelope does not eliminate variance. It preserves decision bandwidth under variance. A narrowing envelope does not eliminate wealth. It makes wealth conditional on uninterrupted stability and favorable ordering, because thresholds sit close enough that ordinary disturbances translate into forced moves.

The divergence across 25–30 years is therefore inevitable under a given trajectory slope. A negative slope produces a system that becomes increasingly sensitive, increasingly present-constrained, and increasingly dependent on favorable sequencing. A positive slope produces a system that becomes less sensitive, less ordering-dependent, and more capable of absorbing clustered shocks without structural damage. Two households can share the same income profile and the same average return profile yet diverge because one accumulates distance and the other accumulates density.

When the horizon extends beyond a single career phase, the system begins to behave less like a set of monthly cash flows and more like an engineered durability profile. The key variables are not the peak values achieved at any point. The key variables are the distances preserved when conditions reverse. A system that reaches a high peak through correlated concentration but cannot prevent forced conversion during reversal does not compound; it oscillates around shrinking distance. A system that grows more slowly but preserves distance through reversals compounds continuity and retains the ability to choose timing.

Stability is architecture. Architecture is governed. Governance determines breakpoint migration. Breakpoint migration determines optionality. Optionality determines life trajectory.

Over decades, configuration compounds more than income. Architecture compounds more than return rate. Stability compounds more than optimism.

About the Author

Mark Ellison writes about structural durability in systems exposed to volatility.

His work focuses on long-horizon stability across financial architecture, career positioning, cognitive resilience, and physical capacity. Rather than treating these domains as separate disciplines, he approaches them as interdependent systems governed by load, margin, buffer depth, and threshold behavior.

The Stability framework examines how fragility accumulates gradually and how disciplined structural calibration preserves optionality across decades. The objective is not optimization for peak outcomes, but preservation of functional continuity under variance.

Money Stability is part of a broader multi-domain stability ecosystem developed under Perennial Publishing, each domain addressing a distinct vector of long-term durability.

The work is designed for readers who prefer structural clarity over motivational rhetoric and long-horizon coherence over short-term intensity.

The Money Stability Series

Money Stability*: How to Build Financial Control in an Unstable World*

(Cornerstone Volume)

Future Titles include:

Liquidity and Runway

Income Stability

Expense Stability